THE PHARISEES AND JESUS

THE PHARISEES AND JESUS

THE STONE LECTURES FOR 1915-16

DELIVERED AT THE PRINCETON
THEOLOGICAL SEMINARY

BY

A. T. ROBERTSON

A.M., D.D., LL.D., D.LITT.

PROFESSOR OF INTERPRETATION OF THE NEW TESTAMENT
IN THE SOUTHERN BAPTIST THEOLOGICAL SEMINARY

AUTHOR OF A 'GRAMMAR OF THE GREEK NEW TESTAMENT IN THE
LIGHT OF HISTORICAL RESEARCH,' 'EPOCHS IN
THE LIFE OF JESUS,' ETC.

Wipf and Stock Publishers
EUGENE, OREGON

Wipf and Stock Publishers
199 West 8th Avenue, Suite 3
Eugene, Oregon 97401

The Pharisees and Jesus
The Stone Lectures for 1915-1916
By Robertson, A.T.
ISBN: 1-57910-289-1
Publication date: October, 1999
Previously published by Charles Scribner's Sons, 1920.

TO

**THE FACULTY AND STUDENTS OF
PRINCETON THEOLOGICAL SEMINARY**

PREFACE

PORTIONS of this volume were delivered as lectures on the L. P. Stone Foundation the last week in February 1916, before the Princeton Theological Seminary. The author recalls with pleasure the kindly interest of Faculty and Students during those days. The lectures have been revised and enlarged and adapted to the purpose of the present volume. It is a gratifying sign of the times that modern Jewish scholars exhibit a friendly spirit towards Jesus and Christianity. It is highly important that Jews and Christians understand each other. That is the best way to appreciate and to admire the good in each other. The treatment of Jesus by the Pharisees and of the Pharisees by Jesus is an inflammable subject for some minds, but it is one that has to be discussed and, indeed, has been discussed with great fidelity. Recent efforts to get a new conception of the Pharisees make it necessary to review the whole problem in the light of the new knowledge. If the story is a sad one, it must be remembered that the facts of history cannot be changed. We must learn the lesson of love and mutual forbearance from the strife of the past. The author does not pose as an absolutely impartial and indifferent student of the

CONTENTS

I. THE PHARISAIC OUTLOOK ON DOCTRINE AND LIFE

SECT.		PAGE
1.	The Importance of Understanding the Pharisees	1
2.	The Alleged Misrepresentation of the Pharisees	4
3.	The Possibility of Treating the Pharisees Fairly	7
4.	A Sketch of the History of the Pharisees up to the Time of Christ	12
5.	The Standing of the Pharisees in the First Century A.D.	17
6.	The Seven Varieties of the Pharisees	23
7.	The Two Schools of Theology	27
8.	The Two Methods of Pharisaic Teaching	28
9.	The Chief Points in Pharisaic Theology	35
10.	The Practice of Pharisaism in Life	43
11.	The Apocalyptists	48

II. THE PHARISAIC RESENTMENT TOWARD JESUS

1.	The Spirit of the Talmud toward Jesus	51
2.	Jewish Hatred Shown in Early Christian Writings	56
3.	The Picture in the Acts of the Apostles	58

THE PHARISEES AND JESUS

SECT.		PAGE
4.	The Story of Pharisaic Hate Common to all the Gospels.	60
5.	Some Friendly Pharisees	63
6.	Presumption against Jesus because of John the Baptist.	65
7.	Grounds of Pharisaic Dislike of Jesus	66
	(1) Assumption of Messianic Authority	66
	(2) Downright Blasphemy	71
	(3) Intolerable Association with Publicans and Sinners	76
	(4) Irreligious Neglect of Fasting	81
	(5) The Devil Incarnate or in league with Beelzebub	83
	(6) A Regular Sabbath Breaker	85
	(7) Utterly Inadequate Signs	90
	(8) Insolent Defiance of Tradition	93
	(9) An Ignorant Impostor	97
	(10) Plotting to Destroy the Temple	102
	(11) High Treason against Cæsar	104

III. THE CONDEMNATION OF THE PHARISEES BY JESUS

1.	Spiritual Blindness	111
2.	Formalism	120
3.	Prejudice	126
4.	Traditionalism	129
5.	Hypocrisy	133
6.	Blasphemy against the Holy Spirit	148
7.	Rejection of God in Rejecting Jesus	151
	List of Important Works	160
	Index	172

THE PHARISEES AND JESUS

CHAPTER I

THE PHARISAIC OUTLOOK ON DOCTRINE AND LIFE

1. *The Importance of Understanding the Pharisees*

THEOLOGICAL controversy is out of harmony with the temper of the twentieth century, but one can by no means understand the life and teachings of Jesus if he is wholly averse to such a topic. The short earthly ministry of our Lord, at most only three and a half years in length (about the duration of an average city pastorate), fairly bristles with the struggle made by the Pharisees to break the power of Christ's popularity with the people. Jesus is challenged at the very start, and is thrown on the defensive by the rabbis, who are the established and accepted religious leaders of the Jewish people. They wish no revolutionary propaganda that will interfere with their hold on the masses. They are jealous of their prerogatives, these men who 'sit on Moses' seat' (Matt. xxiii. 2).[1] The thing to note here is that Jesus recognises the right of the Pharisees to sit upon their places of ecclesiastical eminence. He even commends the general tenor of their instructions : ' All things whatsoever they bid you, these do and observe '

---

[1] 'Επὶ τῆς Μωυσέως ἐκαθέδρας κάθισαν. The aorist here is gnomic or timeless and suits well the hoary traditions of prerogative felt by the Pharisaic incumbents of Mosaic place and power. Note ἐπί, a more formal statement than ἐν would give.

(Matt. xxiii. 3).¹ But Jesus in the very next verse hastens to warn His hearers against the conduct of the Pharisees, 'for they say and do not' (λέγουσιν γὰρ καὶ οὐ ποιοῦσιν). And yet this sharp paradox is not to be taken with the utmost literalness, for not all the acts of the Pharisees were wrong, and not all their teaching is to be commended. But the heart of the criticism of Jesus is thus reached at once. It is the discrepancy between conduct and creed. When presented in this form one is bound to admit that the issue is not a merely antiquarian or academic problem, but concerns every lover and seeker after righteousness in our own day. The term Pharisee has come to signify hypocrisy wherever found. Is it unjust? This we must answer by and by.

The Pharisees are interesting, indeed, from the standpoint of historical study. They are 'the most characteristic manifestation of Palestinian Judaism in the time of Christ' (H. M. Scott in *Hastings' D.C.G.*). They alone of the Jewish parties survived the destruction of the temple and the city. Modern Judaism is immensely indebted to Pharisaism. 'The Pharisees remained, as representing all that was left alive of Judaism.' ² Indeed, Rabbi K. Kohler (*Jewish Encyclopædia*, art. 'Pharisees') says: 'Pharisaism shaped the character of Judaism and the life and thought of the Jew for all the future.' He justified its 'separation' and exclusiveness in that it preserved in the Jew his monotheism in the wreck of the old world and the barbarism of the medieval age.

It is impossible to understand the atmosphere of Christ's earthly life without an adequate knowledge of the Pharisees. They largely created the atmosphere

---

[1] ποιήσατε καὶ τηρεῖτε. The change of tense from the aorist (punctiliar) to the present imperative (linear) shows that Jesus had no objection to the existence of the Pharisees *per se* as religious leaders.
[2] Herford, *Pharisaism*, p. 45.

which the people breathed, and into which Jesus came. Our Lord had to relate His message and mission at once to this dominant theology of his time in Palestine.[1] The people were quick to compare His message with that of the official rabbis, and to express their astonishment at His teaching, ' for he taught them as one having authority and not as their scribes ' (Matt. vii. 29).[2] It is not a question whether we like the Pharisees or not. The historical environment of Jesus in Palestine can now be quite definitely outlined, at least in its broader aspects.[3] On the theological side, the Pharisees occupy far the major part of the space and transcend all other parties in importance, for our knowledge of the historical setting of the teaching of Jesus.

The fidelity of the picture in the Gospels is so manifest, that even Wernle[4] says : ' One thing is certain, that Jesus and His Gospel are intelligible from Judaism alone ; and for this, for Jesus and His relation to Palestinian Judaism, other and more accurate data are available. He appeared in the last dying moments of the theocracy, and before the exclusive rule of the Rabbis which succeeded it Here, it is true, it can be affirmed that only a few decades later the origin of Christianity would be inconceivable.' Certainly no one who knows Wernle's writings will accuse him of being an apologist for Jesus or for Christianity. He is therefore a good antidote for the theory [5]

[1] Bousset, *Jesu Predigt*, p. 32.
[2] The point in ἐξουσίαν is that Jesus possessed the power (authority) of truth and stood on his own feet and spoke it. He felt no call to bolster it up with the decisions of the rabbis.
[3] Cf. Schuerer, *History of the Jewish People in the Time of Christ*, 5 vols. ; Angus, *Environment of Early Christianity*, to go no further.
[4] *Beginnings of Christianity*, vol. i. pp. 33 f.
[5] See, for instance, A. Drews, *Die Zeugnisse für die Geschichtlichkeit Jesu* (1911), *The Christ Myth* (1911) ; W. B. Smith, *Der Christliche Jesus* (1906), *The Pre-Christian Jesus* (1906) ; J. M. Robertson, *Pagan Christs* (1903). But one of their own school, F. C. Conybeare in his *Historical Christ* (1914), has produced a crushing reply to the whole absurdity. See also the whole matter surveyed by Case, *The Historicity of Jesus* (1912), and by Thorburn, *Jesus the Christ: Historical or Mythical* (1912).

that denies the historicity of Jesus, and seeks to dissipate all the evidence into the mist and myth of subjective imagination. The sharpness of the contrast between Jesus and the Pharisees in so many fundamental matters argues for the reality of the controversy, and the date before the destruction of Jerusalem as the time for the picture drawn in the Gospels. It is a pathetic outcome of Schweitzer's *Quest of the Historical Jesus* (1910, p. 401), when he laments: 'We can find no designation which expresses what he is for us.' He has tried to overthrow 'the modern Jesus' of theology by the 'true historical Jesus,' but he is so confused by the dust of his own learning that he cannot recognise Jesus when he sees Him. The Gospels in a wonderful way preserve and reproduce the colouring of the life in Galilee and Jerusalem, while Pharisee and Sadducee shared the power, and were full of jealousy of each other, while the Palestinian Jew still felt his superiority in privilege over the Jew of the Diaspora, while the middle wall of partition between Jew and Gentile was still unbroken and seemed unbreakable.

2. *The Alleged Misrepresentation of the Pharisees*

It is now a common remark in books about the Pharisees that they are not treated fairly in the New Testament. The usually fair Rabbi Kohler [1] says: 'No true estimate of the character of the Pharisees can be obtained from the New Testament writings, which take a polemical attitude toward them, nor from Josephus, who, writing for Roman readers and in view of the Messianic expectation of the Pharisees, represents the latter as a philosophical sect.' But Josephus was himself a Pharisee of the liberal sort. However, Oesterley (*The Books of the Apocrypha*, pp. 136 f.) notes that besides comparing the Pharisees to the Stoics

---

[1] *Jewish Encyclopædia* (art. 'Pharisees').

THE PHARISAIC OUTLOOK

(*Vita*, § 2) and the Essenes with Pythagoreans (*Ant.*, bk. xv. ch. x. § 4), Josephus apparently wrote more about the Pharisees in a paragraph which is lost from the *War*, bk. ii. ch. viii. § 14. His account is certainly incomplete, besides its Hellenising basis. Certainly Paul had been a Pharisee and knew intimately the doctrines and practices of the Pharisees. And yet Herford [1] bluntly says : ' Paul's presentation of Pharisaic Judaism is, in consequence, at its best a distortion, at its worst a fiction.' Surely one cannot forget that this same Paul was once the pride of Pharisaism and the heroic champion of Pharisaic Judaism, in its apparently triumphant conflict with the heresy of Christianity. Montefiore [2] puts the case against Paul much more mildly when he says : ' I am, however, inclined to think that even in 50 Rabbinic Judaism was a better, happier, and more noble religion than one might imagine from the writings of the Apostle.' Herford [3] also pointedly charges Jesus with not being able to comprehend Judaism. ' And alike to Christian and Jew, it is almost impossible to comprehend the religion of the other. Even Jesus could not do it.' Herford in particular takes up the phrase, ' Scribes and Pharisees, hypocrites,' and adds : [4] ' That such a statement should be made of the Pharisees is to Jews hard to endure,' as hard, he argues, as for Christians to stand this sentence in the Talmud : [5] ' Jesus practised magic and led astray and deceived Israel,' or the phrase about Jesus in the Mishna, ' the sinner of Israel.' And Wernle [6] ruthlessly brushes aside Jesus as an interpreter of Pharisaism in the almost brutal words : ' It was His incomplete knowledge of the law which was in this point the cause of an entire deception on the part of Jesus. . . . The

---

[1] *Pharisaism*, p. 191.   [2] *Judaism and St. Paul*, p. 87.
[3] *Pharisaism*, p. 171.   [4] *Ibid.*, p. 115. Cf. b. *Sanh*. 107b.
[5] Treatise *Sotah* : ch. ix. gives the earliest instance of it.
[6] *Beginnings of Christianity*, vol. i. pp. 90 f.

law necessitated the existence of the scribes, the murderers of Jesus. But all this Jesus concealed from Himself throughout His life on earth. . . . The converse of Jesus' positive attitude towards the law is His uncompromising rejection of Pharisaism. He is so unsparing, so entirely without any exception, that the very name of Pharisee has become a term of abuse for all ages.' Herford,[1] it should be added, does draw a distinction between the method of Jesus and that of Paul : ' Paul condemned Pharisaism in theory, while Jesus condemned it in practice.' The attack of Jesus was more concrete and hurt most, and has lasted till to-day. We see, then, that moderate Jewish writers, like Kohler and Montefiore, and some non-Jewish writers like Herford and Wernle, expressly claim that Jesus, Paul, and New Testament writers generally have distinctly misunderstood and misrepresented Pharisaism. The closing chapter of Herford's book on ' Pharisaism ' is entitled *Pharisaism as a Spiritual Religion*. He admits [2] that ' it is easy to make Pharisaism appear ridiculous, a mere extravagance of punctilious formalism,' and claims that ' Pharisaism is entitled to be judged according to what the Pharisees themselves meant by it, and its worth to be established by what they found in it.' This claim has a large element of justice in it, but Pharisaism, like Christianity, must submit to the judgment of all men, the universal conscience. Certainly it is true that Christians should be willing to look at the facts about Pharisaism. It is probably true, as Montefiore [3] charges, that many of the modern antagonists of Rabbinic Judaism ' have been somewhat lacking in first-hand knowledge.' On the other hand, Montefiore [4] frankly admits that ' the Jewish scholar has hitherto shown little capacity for appreciating Paul,'

[1] *Pharisaism*, p. 191. [2] *Ibid.*, p. 107.
[3] *Judaism and St. Paul*, p. 7. [4] *Ibid.*, p. 9.

THE PHARISAIC OUTLOOK

or Jesus, as he would freely add, though he does claim that the standpoint of a modern Jew towards Jesus should be of interest to Christians.[1] At any rate, it is perfectly clear that the subject of the Pharisee demands reinvestigation in the light of the repeated charges of unfairness in the New Testament pictures, and in particular on the part of Jesus Himself.

3. *The Possibility of Treating the Pharisees Fairly*

It can be said at once that it is not easy to do this. Oesterley and Box (*The Religion and Worship of the Synagogue*, p. ix.) indeed say that 'the time is hardly ripe for a full discussion of the important issues' connected with the Pharisees. But surely we cannot agree that it is impossible for Christian scholars to be just even to the enemies of Jesus. It is not necessary, however, for one to become a blind champion of the Pharisees in order to do them justice. This is precisely what Herford has done in his *Pharisaism*. In order to do 'justice to the Pharisees' (p. 6), he conceives it necessary to divest himself of Christianity and not to judge Pharisaism 'by the standard of the Christian religion,' as Oesterley and Box do in *The Religion and Worship of the Synagogue*. That is to claim that 'no one but a Jew, of whom it may be said that the Talmud runs in his blood, can fully realise the spiritual meaning of Pharisaism' (p. 3). But it is merely special pleading to assert that no one has a right to pass judgment upon a system of thought or upon a religion save the devotees of the system. That is the plea of the Christian Scientist, of the Mormon, of the Buddhist, of the Mohammedan, but surely not of the enlightened Christian, who stands in the open and invites comparison between Christ and all other teachers in the world. Herford poses as the

[1] *The Religious Teaching of Jesus*, p. 9.

pioneer in the business of treating the Pharisees fairly.[1] 'Something was still left to be done, by way of treating the Pharisees fairly, that is, without either contempt or condescension; and that "something" I have tried to do.' Certainly he has set before himself a laudable ambition, but he proceeds to boost the Pharisees by depreciating Jesus while disclaiming it. 'I will yield to no one,' he says,[2] 'in my reverence for Jesus; He is to me simply the greatest man that ever lived in regard to His spiritual nature. Some may think that too little to say; others may think it too much.' He adds (p. 125), 'I do not contend that all the Pharisees, or any of them, were the equals of Jesus in spiritual depth.' Suffer another word from Herford:[3] 'He was really rejected, so far at all events as the Pharisees were concerned, because He undermined the authority of the Torah, and endangered the religion founded upon it. That Jesus really did so is beyond dispute.' Once more (p. 146) Herford says: 'Torah and Jesus could not remain in harmony. The two were fundamentally incompatible. And the Pharisees being determined to "abide by the things they had learned," viz., Torah, were necessarily turned into opponents of Jesus.' Thus does Herford justify the Pharisees at the expense of Jesus, as a dangerous heretic who had to be put down in order to save the religion of the Jews. Herford calls this treating the Pharisees 'fairly.' What shall we say of his treatment of Jesus?

Apart from the matter of prejudice on both sides of the problem of the Pharisees, we are bound to make serious inquiry about the sources of our knowledge of the subject. We have already seen that Herford rules out Jesus and Paul as witnesses. Montefiore appeals to modern criticism as justifying the most cautious

[1] *Pharisaism*, pp. vi. f. [2] *Ibid.*, p. 114.
[3] *Ibid.*, p. 143.

use of the Gospels and Epistles of Paul,[1] though he finds himself more at home in the atmosphere of the Synoptic Gospels than in that of the Gospel of John and Paul's Epistles (*ibid.*, p. 8). He sees no essential reason why Jews and Christians cannot understand one another just as learned Christians have written just presentations of Buddhism and Confucianism (p. 3). He recognises, however, that the Jew will seek to show the superiority of the Talmud to the Gospels, since ' the Jew has been told over and over again of the immense superiority of the teaching of the New Testament over the Old ' (p. 7).

If we let the ancient Pharisee speak for himself, as he surely has the right to do, we are not without resources, apart from Josephus who must be considered, in spite of Kohler's protest quoted above. In particular we find the Pharisaic teaching in the *Testaments of the Twelve Patriarchs*, certainly in those portions which are clearly pre-Christian, though Charles would place all these writings before Christ. Charles[2] has a very high estimate of this collection of sayings, and says : ' Their ethical teaching, which is indefinitely higher than that of the Old Testament, is yet its true spiritual child, and helps to bridge the chasm that divides the ethics of the Old and New Testaments.' Some scholars, Plummer, for instance, will not admit that these portions of the *Testaments* that come so near the level of the New Testament in some points, are earlier than the Christian era. Shailer Matthews (Hastings' one vol. B.D., p. 40) dates the Testaments in the first and second centuries A.D., and says that ' it is full of Christian interpolations.' But at any rate we find here the view of some of the Pharisees about the time of Christ. The Psalms of Solomon, which belong to the period B.C. 70 to 40 A.D.

---

[1] *The Religious Teaching of Jesus*, pp. 11 f.
[2] *Testaments of the Twelve Patriarchs*, p. 17.

and were written by a Pharisee, voice bitter antagonism toward the Sadducees and justify the downfall of the Maccabean dynasty. The Apocalypse of Esra or Second Esdras was written shortly after the destruction of Jerusalem and 'is the most complete expression of Pharisaic pessimism.' It is thus possible to get an inside view of the Pharisaism of the time, and to compare it with the pictures in Josephus and the New Testament.

But the great storehouse of Pharisaic teaching is in the Talmud and the Midrash. We may let Herford [1] state the case for Pharisaism here : ' In the Talmud is contained the main source for the knowledge of what Pharisaism meant ; because it was made the storehouse in which all, or nearly all, that was held to be valuable in the Tradition of the Elders, the explicit religion of the Torah, was stored up. There is a huge literature contemporary with the Talmud, to which the general name of Midrash is given ; all of it is traditional, and all of it bears on the religion of the Torah, in one way or another. This is the written deposit of Pharisaism, the mark which it has left upon the literature of the world. It is there, and not in the writings of those who did not understand its ideals or share its hopes, that its real meaning can alone be found.' Here we seem to have struck bottom at last. But, unfortunately, the Talmud in its written form is much later than the time of Jesus. The Mishna or Second Law belongs to the period 210 A.D. This writing down of the tradition of the elders or comments on the law came to be in turn ' a code of the law for the guidance of the Jews ' (Herford, *Pharisaism*, p. 52). ' The Mishnah became, in its turn, the subject of study in the Rabbinical schools ' (*ibid.*, p. 53). Then the comments of the rabbis on the Mishna were written down, and were called Gemara (completion)

Pharisaism, pp. 54 f.

THE PHARISAIC OUTLOOK

There were two centres when the Gemara was written out, one in Palestine and one in Babylonia. The Talmud is the Midrash plus the Gemara. Hence we have the Palestinian Talmud and the Babylonian Talmud with the same Midrash, but a separate Gemara. We can see at once that it is a precarious matter to appeal to these late comments (both Midrash and Gemara) as a certain proof of the Pharisaic teaching in the first century A.D. It is for this reason that Montefiore [1] says in all candour: 'The greatest caution is necessary in using the Rabbinical literature to illustrate—whether by way of contrast or parallel—the statements and teachings in the Synoptic Gospels. . . . You can hardly count up the number of rules about the Sabbath in the Midrash and say, there is what the average Jew or Gentile in A.D. 29 was expected to observe.' Certainly we know more of Palestine and of the Jews than we once did. In fact, we know entirely too much to be as dogmatic as Herford in his special plea for the Pharisees. Montefiore [2] says there were many 'Judaisms of the first century,' and adds: 'And of Palestinian or early Rabbinical Judaism it may be said, that we realise better the limits of our knowledge; we realise how meagre is its literary remains; and we realise how the purest Rabbinical Judaism of 50 A.D., whether in doctrine or in the type of the average believer which it produced, may not have been wholly the same as the Rabbinical Judaism of 500 A.D.' This is well said. It is to be remembered also about the New Testament writers that they *assume* a knowledge of the Pharisees and nowhere give full details about their tenets. The background has to be depicted largely by implication. The lines have to be filled in to avoid undue emphasis. Josephus certainly toned down his picture to please the Romans. He does

---

[1] *The Religious Teaching of Jesus*, p. 10.
[2] *Judaism and St. Paul*, p. 4.

not mention the Messianic hope of the Pharisees. As to the Talmud, Thomson [1] says that the lateness of the Gemara, which has most to tell about the Pharisees, 'renders the evidence deduced from the Talmudic statements of little value.' He adds: 'Even the Mishna, which came into being only a century after the fall of the Jewish state, shows traces of exaggeration and modification of facts.' And yet it is possible to look at Jesus and the Pharisees side by side, and to see the facts and to tell the truth about them.

4. *A Sketch of the History of the Pharisees up to the Time of Christ*

The first mention of the Pharisees by name is by Josephus, *Antiquities*, bk. xiii. ch. vii. § 9: 'At this time there were three sects among the Jews, who had different opinions concerning human actions; one was called the sect of the Pharisees, another the sect of the Sadducees, and the other the sect of the Essenes.' By 'at this time' Josephus means the time of Jonathan Maccabæus, whose career he is describing. Jonathan succeeded Judas Maccabæus, and was the leader of the Jews in the struggle for religious liberty and political independence during the years B.C. 161-143. But Josephus tells us something of the origin of these Jewish sects. The next time that he mentions the Pharisees and Sadducees is in connection with the reign of John Hyrcanus I. (B.C. 135-106), where [2] he refers to his previous mention of the Pharisees, 'as we have informed you already.' The Pharisees were so hostile to the possession of both the civil and the religious power by Hyrcanus that finally Eleazar, one of the Pharisees, said to Hyrcanus: 'Since thou desirest to know the truth, if thou wilt be righteous in earnest, lay down the

[1] 'Pharisees' in *International Standard Bible Encyclopedia*.
[2] *Ant.*, bk. xiii. ch. x. §§ 5-6.

THE PHARISAIC OUTLOOK

high priesthood, and content thyself with the civil government of the people.' When pressed for his reason for that demand, Eleazar said : ' We have heard it from old men, that thy mother had been a captive under the reign of Antiochus Epiphanes.' This unforgivable insult implied that Hyrcanus was a bastard, son of an unknown stranger, to whom his mother had given herself, and not a true son of Aaron. This pretext angered Hyrcanus still more, with the result that he left the Pharisees, to whose party he belonged, and went over to that of the Sadducees. This incident is very suggestive, and throws light in various directions. It shows that the Pharisees and Sadducees had been in existence for some time, and are in clear-cut opposition. The Pharisees wish the high priesthood to be separate from the civil government and are opposed to the union of Church and State. The Maccabees were not Zadokites, though priests. The resentment of the Assidean purists had been shown against Judas, and led to the welcome given the treacherous Alcimus with such dire results (1 Macc. vii. 9). The Pharisees here appear more as a religious sect and less as a political party. They wish, of course, for the high priest to be a Pharisee, and for the Pharisees to have control of the religious life of the people. The Sadducees are rejoiced to have Hyrcanus on their side, and make no protest against his possession of both the civil and religious leadership. But the Sadducees are at bottom a political party, while the Pharisees are a religious party, though each make use of both elements to carry their points. The Pharisees are now the party of the opposition with the Sadducees in authority, and they show their resentment in vigorous fashion. They fight Alexander Jannæus so bitterly, that in a rage he has many of the Pharisees in Jerusalem slain; according to Josephus :[1] 'He ordered about

[1] *Ant.*, bk. xiii. ch. xiv. § 2.

eight hundred of them to be crucified ; and while they were living, he ordered the throats of their children and wives to be cut before their eyes.' Already before this, ' at a festival which was then celebrated, when he stood upon the altar, the nation rose upon him and pelted him with citrons.' [1] Evidently the Pharisees have kept their leadership of the people, though they had lost the king and high priest. The Pharisees resented the Hellenic name ' Alexander,' which Jannæus had as well as the title of ' king,' since he was not of the Davidic line. Besides, a high priest was not allowed to marry a widow, and yet he had married the widow of his brother Aristobulus I. Alexander Jannæus learned his lesson, and before his death advised [2] his wife to ' put some of her authority into the hands of the Pharisees, for,' he told her, ' they had great authority over the Jews.' ' Promise them also that thou wilt do nothing without them in the affairs of the kingdom.' Salome Alexandra took her husband's advice, and made their son John Hyrcanus II., ' rather than Aristobulus, high priest, because he was the elder, but much more because he cared not to meddle with politics, and permitted the Pharisees to do everything.' [3] Josephus facetiously adds : ' So she had the name of the regent, but the Pharisees had the authority.' It was a veritable millennium for the Pharisees. The Sadducees found an ally in Aristobulus (Aristobulus II.). Upon the death of Salome Alexandra the kingship also passed to Hyrcanus, but Aristobulus made war upon Hyrcanus his brother, with the result that Hyrcanus surrendered the kingship to Aristobulus and kept the high priesthood.[4] This compromise was due to the mild disposition of Hyrcanus, and after all suited very well both the Pharisees and the Sadducees, for each party had what it cared most

[1] *Ant.*, bk. xiii. ch. xiii. § 5. [3] *Ibid.*, ch. xv. § 5.
[2] *Ibid.*, ch. xvi. § 2. [4] *Ibid.*, bk. xiv. ch. i. § 1.

about, the one the religious leadership, the other the political.

The 'ifs' of history are always interesting. If the Idumean upstart, Antipater, had not turned up in Jerusalem and stirred up the gentle Hyrcanus to try to regain the civil power,[1] the after history of the Jews might have been very different. Antipater was like the modern political 'boss' who holds no office, and yet selects all who do hold such positions of power. He is the invisible government. Antipater is concerned about the civil rule which Aristobulus has. He selects Hyrcanus as his tool because he is the more pliable of the two brothers. Antipater is neither Pharisee nor Sadducee, and has neither politics nor religion, but uses both to further his own ambition for power. So he plays the Pharisees against the Sadducees in his effort to oust Aristobulus from the kingship and to restore it to Hyrcanus, whom he can manage. He makes Hyrcanus appeal to Aretas king of Arabia for help. This fratricidal contest, with the Arabs as arbiters, furnishes Pompey with a plausible excuse to come to Jerusalem on his way back from Armenia against Tigranes, and to assert the power of Rome in the dispute, with the result, after vacillation and trickery on the part of Aristobulus, that Jerusalem is captured, Aristobulus is taken captive to Rome, and Hyrcanus is left high priest, but not king.[2] The Pharisees are left where they were, but the Sadducees are worsted. This was B.C. 63, and the glorious days of Maccabean independence are over. The Roman yoke has now been placed upon the Jews.

Roman wars play a part in the history of the Pharisees. Upon the defeat and death of Pompey, Hyrcanus and Antipater find themselves on the side of the vanquished. Julius Cæsar reversed the policy of Pompey, and restored

[1] *Ant.*, §§ 2-4.   [2] *Ibid.*, chs. ii.-v.

the party of the Sadducees to power by offering the high priesthood to Aristobulus. But Aristobulus and his son Alexander were slain, and only Antigonus, another son, was left.[1]

Another turn in the wheel of fortune for the Pharisees came when Antipater went down to Egypt to help Julius Cæsar against Mithridates of Pontus, and did it so successfully that Cæsar felt that he owed his victory to Antipater, and as a result made him his personal representative in Palestine, with Hyrcanus as high priest.[2] Thus the Pharisees are back again in ecclesiastical power. Antipater is at last supreme in Palestine.

However, the death of Cæsar and the victory of Antony and Octavius over Brutus and Cassius left Herod, Antipater's son and prospective son-in-law of Hyrcanus, on the side of the defeated party.[3] But Herod finally won the favour of Antony, ruler of the East, and was appointed Tetrarch with Hyrcanus as high priest. Thus the Pharisees retained their hold till the Parthians[4] came and set up Antigonus as king and high priest in Jerusalem, and so reinstated the Sadducees in power. Hyrcanus is mutilated, his ears being cut off by order of Antigonus, so that he could not be high priest any more, and was made the captive of the Parthians.[5]

In despair Herod fled to Aretas in Arabia and then to Egypt, in search of Antony, and found him in Rome. Here Antony and Octavius, to Herod's surprise and joy, have him appointed King of Judea by the Senate. This was in B.C. 40, but it took him three years to secure the kingdom from Antigonus and the Parthians.[6]

Henceforth the high priesthood is in the hands of Herod the Great, who appoints his puppets to office.[7]

---

[1] *Ant.*, ch. vii. § 4.
[2] *Ibid.*, chs. xi-xiii.
[3] *Ibid.*, ch. xiii. § 10.
[7] *Ibid.*, bk. xv. ch. i. § 4.
[3] *Ibid.*, bk. xiv. ch. viii.
[4] *Ibid.*, ch. xiii.
[6] *Ibid.*, chs. xiv.-xv.

I.] THE PHARISAIC OUTLOOK 17

When the Romans make a province instead of a vassal kingdom out of Palestine, they themselves appoint the high priest.[1] In the ministry of Jesus the Sadducees control the high priesthood. The chief priests are Sadducees. Both Annas and Caiaphas are Sadducees. This long struggle for power made the bitterness between these two parties very sharp.

5. *The Standing of the Pharisees in the First Century A.D.*

The brief outline just given of the struggle of the Pharisees for power shows that they had won the sympathy and support of the masses of the people. This was due mainly to the fact that the Pharisees were the heirs and successors of the Hasidim or Assideans of the Maccabean books, the Loyalists or Puritans who resisted the efforts of Antiochus Epiphanes and the Hellenising high priests, Jason and Menelaus, to compel the Jews to adopt Greek customs, and even to worship Zeus and eat swine's flesh. It is a tragic story as it is told with simple power in 1 Macc. i.-ii. The revolt of Mattathias, and the long struggle under Judas and Jonathan, with final victory under Simon, is one of the heroic passages of history. It is clear that the Pharisees carried over the attitude of this patriotic party toward Hellenism, and that the Sadducees became the heirs of the Hellenisers. Aristobulus I. (B.C. 106) was a Sadducee, and was known as the Phil-hellene, so that one of the Maccabees actually went over to the standpoint of the Hellenisers, after the fight against the Hellenisers had been won by the Maccabees. Shades of Mattathias and of Judas! The Sadducees were more hospitable to foreign influences of all sorts, while the Pharisees stood

[1] *Ant.*, bk. xx. ch. ix. § 1.

firmly by the tradition of the elders and the integrity of Judaism.[1]

Certainly the roots of Pharisaism run back into the past, even beyond the Hasidim. Indeed, the Pharisees trace their origin in principle back to Ezra. Rabbi Lakish (b. *Succ.* xx. ª) says: 'When the Torah was forgotten, Ezra came up from Babylon and re-established it; when it was forgotten again, Hillel came up from Babylon and re-established it; and when it was forgotten again, R. Hija and his sons came up from Babylon and re-established it.' Herford[2] claims that 'while no one would say that Ezra was a Pharisee, it is true that he was a spiritual ancestor of the Pharisees, more than of any other element in post-exilic Judaism.' He adds: 'Pharisaism alone was the result of his work; and Pharisaism alone survived, to carry down through the centuries the spiritual treasure of Israel.' To this last statement I should certainly object, for I agree with Paul that Christianity is the true Israel of promise, and it is a heavy load on Ezra to hold him responsible for all the traditions and practices of the Pharisees. Herford (p. 9) even says that, 'if Ezra had not come, it is conceivable, and indeed highly probable, that Judaism would have disappeared altogether.' But it is true beyond a doubt that the synagogue and the scribes, the powerful agencies in the hands of the Pharisees, were used to make the law an effective guard to keep the Jews from again going after strange gods, as before the Babylonian Captivity. 'But before faith came, we were kept in ward under the law ($\hat{v}\pi\grave{o}$ $\nu\acute{o}\mu o\nu$ $\grave{\epsilon}\phi\rho o\upsilon\rho o\acute{\upsilon}\mu\epsilon\theta a$),[3] shut up ($\sigma\upsilon\gamma\kappa\lambda\epsilon\iota\acute{o}\mu\epsilon\nu o\iota$)[4] unto the faith which should afterwards be revealed' (Gal. iii. 23). So then the middle wall of partition did serve a good pur-

---

[1] Josephus, *Ant.*, bk. xiii. ch. xi.   [2] *Pharisaism*, p. 6.
[3] Note imperfect tense, the long process of confinement.
[4] Shut together and the Gentiles shut out.

pose, hard as it was to batter down this mark of hate towards the Gentiles, as it came to be (cf. Eph. ii. 14-17).

The scribes so often mentioned in connection with the Pharisees in the Gospels were a profession, not a party or sect. They were nearly all Pharisees, though some of them were Sadducees. So the scribes (copyists of the law, then students, teachers, exponents of the law, doctors or lawyers) taught the law from the Pharisaic standpoint, and helped to make Pharisaism popular and powerful. As we have seen in the time of Jesus, the Romans gave the Sadducean high priest the chief power in internal affairs of Jewish administration.[1] The small Sadducean aristocracy had great power, but the Pharisees had representatives in the Sanhedrin (cf. Acts v. 34; xxiii. 6), and were able to exercise great power with the people.[2]

The Sadducees claimed affiliation with the priests and the Pharisees with the scribes.[3] The Sadducees were a priestly aristocracy of blood, while the Pharisees were an aristocracy of learning.[4] Kohler[5] calls the Pharisees the party of progress, and the Sadducees the party of reaction, but there are two sides to that question. The Sadducees were narrower than the Pharisees in their insistence upon the law of Moses as alone binding, in opposition to the Pharisaic traditions, but the Sadducees, on the other hand, were more open to the Greek and Roman life around them, almost Hellenisers, and ridiculed the Pharisees for their ceremonial punctilios about the Gentiles.

The Pharisees, though made finally an aggressive political party from necessity, were at bottom a brotherhood with oath of initiation and rules for life that dis-

[1] Josephus, *Ant.*, bk. xx. ch. ix. § 1.
[2] *Ibid.*, bk. xviii. ch. i. § 4.
[3] Schuerer, *Jewish People in Time of Jesus Christ*, div. ii. vol. ii. p. 9.
[4] Kohler in *Jewish Encycl.* [5] *Ibid.*

tinguished them from other Jews. The old *hasidhim* were 'saints' like the English Puritans or the Cameronians in Scotland who would have none of William of Orange, because he was not a 'covenanted' king.[1] The Pharisees, *perushim* (from *parash*, פָּרַשׁ, to separate),[2] those who had organised themselves into brotherhoods (*habhuroth*) in order to study the law and to obey its precepts. The *habhurim* or neighbours required an oath of fidelity in the presence of three other *habhurim*. This vow of initiation required the ideal of Levitical ceremonial[3] purity, the avoidance of the *'am-ha-'arets* ('the ignorant and careless boor' who disregarded the Levitical requirements), the payment of tithes, the regard for other people's property, and respect for vows. These Pharisaic brotherhoods admitted women to their membership, and made proselytes as Jesus said : 'Ye compass sea and land to make one proselyte' (Matt. xxiii. 15). But membership was voluntary, and certificate of good character was required as well as a period of probation. The number of the Pharisees in Palestine in the time of Jesus was about six thousand, and they were scattered all over the country, though Jerusalem in Judea was headquarters.

They met Jesus in Jerusalem, in Galilee, in Perea, in Decapolis. They are not so powerful in the government of the country as the Herodians and the Sadducees,

---

[1] Thomson in *Intern. Stand. Bible Encycl.*

[2] However, it is only fair to say that Leszynsky (*Die Sadduzäer*, p. 25) makes out a plausible case for the view that 'Pharisee' does not mean 'separate,' but 'expounder' or 'interpreter,' since the root *p-r-sh* means both to 'interpret' and to 'separate.' He finds the term for 'separate oneself' used in *Niddah* iv. 2 of the Sadducees in a disparaging sense, and he quotes Hillel (*Aboth* ii. 4) as saying: 'Separate not thyself from the congregation.' Hence he believes that Josephus (*War*, bk. ii. ch. viii. § 14) rightly describes Pharisees thus: 'They are those who seem to explain the laws with accuracy. Oesterley (*The Books of the Apocrypha*, pp. 131 f.) is completely convinced by these arguments and changes his former view in *The Religion and Worship of the Synagogue*. This is what the scribes (mostly Pharisees) did. But I still doubt this explanation for Pharisees.

[3] Cf. Lev. xix. 18.

THE PHARISAIC OUTLOOK

though certainly they had a strong representation in the Sanhedrin (Acts xxiii. 6-9), for they were able to defeat the effort of the Sadducees to injure Paul as Gamaliel had done about Peter and John (Acts v. 34 f.). But the people accepted the Pharisees as the orthodox interpreters of Judaism as opposed to the Sadducees, Herodians, Essenes, and for a while the Zealots.

We have seen how the Sadducees stood in bold outline, few and powerful priestly aristocrats, against the Pharisees. Two of the other parties were offshoots of the Pharisaic movement (the Essenes and the Zealots). Thomson (*Intern. Stand. Bible Encycl.*) thinks that the Essenes were descendents of the Assidean purists, who fled to the desert to escape the tyranny of Antiochus Epiphanes (1 Macc. ii. 27), and who lived on there in protest even against the Maccabeans and the Pharisees. They were Pharisees run to seed or carried to the nth degree, and the mystics of Judaism with a dash of Persian astrology and Greek philosophy and the asceticism of some of the other mystery-religions. The Zealots,[1] on the other hand, were the fanatics of the Pharisees, who grew tired of the slow opposition of the body of the Pharisees to Roman oppression and Sadducean subserviency These Zealots[2] precipitated the war with Rome (see Josephus' *War*, v. i.), and thus played the decisive part in the culmination of political Judaism. They were scornful of the time-serving Pharisees who were ready, many of them, to make peace with the Romans as Josephus did. The Herodians, on the other hand, opposed all the other parties in the insistence that Judea should have one of the Herods as king after the deposition of Archelaus. They have power even during

[1] See Josephus' account of the origin of the Zealots by Judas, the Gaulonite, as a protest against Roman taxation. *Ant.*, bk. xviii. ch. i. § 1.

[2] Simon Zelotes, one of the Twelve Apostles, belonged to this party. There were no Pharisees, Sadducees, Essenes, or Herodians among the Twelve.

the procuratorship of Pontius Pilate. In the life of Christ all these parties are active and aggressive in public life, save the Essenes, who lived in the wilderness apart from the whirl of politics and theology. With the destruction of Jerusalem all vanish save the Pharisees, who become practically the nation. Pharisaism after 70 A.D. may be said to be the religion of official Judaism, and it has remained so ever since. First it gathered round the oral law or Midrash, as the interpretation of the law. Then the Mishna was the interpretation of the oral law. Then the Gemara explained the Mishna. The Talmud has now become the actual Jewish Bible far more than the Old Testament.

The Pharisees in the time of Jesus have all the pride of a religious inheritance. They have Abraham to their father as all the Jews did, but their knowledge of the law and ceremonial punctiliousness placed them far above other Jews and all Gentiles. 'This multitude ('*am-ha-'arets*, people of the land) that knoweth not the law are accursed' (John. vii. 49), the Pharisees scornfully retort to the soldiers in defence of their hostility to Jesus. A Pharisee is not allowed to eat at the table of another Pharisee, if his wife is one of ' the people of the land ' ('*am-ha-'arets*). He must not sell to one of the '*am-ha-'arets* or have any association with any of them. One thinks at once of the caste system of India. The *origin* of this attitude is seen in the description of the heathen and half-heathen people of Palestine, in distinction from the Jews who came back from Babylon (cf. Ezra ix. 1 f. ; x. 2, 11 ; Neh. x. 28-31). They brand as 'publicans and sinners' not merely the really wicked, but all who are not 'righteous' like themselves. From the Pharisaic standpoint there were two great classes of society, the righteous and the sinners. Their spiritual pride is seen to perfection in the prayer of the Pharisee in the temple in

Jesus' parable of the Pharisee and the Publican in Luke xviii. We see it also all through the Psalms of Solomon, where condemnation is invoked upon the Sadducees and all others (sinners) who are not Pharisees.[1] In Luke xviii. 13 the publican describes himself as 'the sinner' ($\tau\hat{\varphi}$ $\dot{\alpha}\mu\alpha\rho\tau\omega\lambda\hat{\varphi}$), as the Pharisee referred to him contemptuously as 'this publican.' The Pharisees are the exponents of official Judaism, the custodians of the Torah, the hope of the future, and have accepted explanations for all scripture and for every problem of life.

6. *The Seven Varieties of the Pharisees*

The Pharisees were not at one with themselves save in opposition to everybody else. There is no logical place to stop in the business of Pharisaic seclusiveness when once it is started. The line was drawn against the Gentiles, against the '*am-ha-'arets* among the Jews, against the publicans and sinners, against the Sadducees, and then against some of the Pharisees themselves. The Talmud itself gives the seven varieties of the Pharisees, and all but the last one are afflicted with hypocrisy, the sin that Jesus so vigorously denounces, and that stirs the modern apologists of Pharisaism to such rage. Even the Psalms of Solomon are full of denunciations of hypocrisy. Thomson (*Intern. Stand. Bible Encycl.*) argues that hypocrisy was 'a new sin, a sin only possible in a spiritual religion, a religion in which morality and worship were closely related.' Certainly, the true Judaism was not hypocrisy, but it is remarkable that the Psalms of Solomon (a Pharisaic book), the New Testament, and Talmud (the Pharisaic Bible), all give hypocrisy as the chief sin of the Pharisees. Herford[2] admits that the Pharisaic theory of the Torah ' could, and in some cases did, lead to that mere formal-

[1] Cf. Psalms of Sol. ii. 38-41; xiii. 5-11; xiv. 1; xvii. 16, 26.
[2] *Pharisaism*, pp. 105 f.

ism and hypocrisy which have been charged upon the Pharisees as a class.' He claims that 'such formalism and hypocrisy were only the perversion of Pharisaism and not inherent in it.' This is one of the points to examine. Meanwhile the seven types of Pharisees are pictured in the Talmud [1] itself.

(a) The 'Shoulder' Pharisee. This type wears his good deeds on his shoulders, and is very punctilious in his observance of the Torah, traditions and all, from expediency, not from principle. He finds that Pharisaism pays one in the increased reputation for purity. As Jesus said, they did their righteousness 'to be seen of men' ($\pi\rho\grave{o}s$ $\tau\grave{o}$ $\theta\epsilon\alpha\theta\hat{\eta}\nu\alpha\iota$), not for the moral and spiritual worth of the act.

(b) The 'wait-a-little' Pharisee. He always has an excuse for not doing the good deed just now, like the Spanish proverb 'Mañana' ('to-morrow'). One is reminded at once of the man whom Jesus invited to follow him (Luke ix. 57-60), but who excused himself on the ground that he must first go and bury his father. We know from Tobit vi. 14 ('They have no other son to bury them') that the idea of this man (probably a Pharisee) was to go and stay with his father till he was dead and buried, and then to come and follow Jesus. Another man wanted first to bid farewell to those at home (Luke ix. 61 f.). Thus the Pharisee preserved his creed at the expense of his conduct.

(c) The 'bruised' or 'bleeding' Pharisee. This Pharisee is too pious to look at a woman, and so shuts his eyes if he fears one is coming, and stumbles against a wall, and makes the blood flow from his face. He is anxious that the blood shall be seen in order to gain credit for his piety. One is reminded of the beggars to-day who mutilate themselves to arouse pity. In

[1] The seven sorts of Pharisees are described in the Babylonian Talmud (*Sotah*, 22b).

Sotah, f. **xxi**. 2, we read : ' Foolish saints, crafty villains, sanctimonious women, and self-afflicting Pharisees are the destroyers of the world.' There are plenty of parallels in the Brahmanism of India to-day and in types of Roman Catholicism. There were (and are) men who leer at women with lustful eyes (cf. Christ's denunciation in Matt. v. 28), but these Pharisees looked on women as the personification of evil. The disciples of Jesus were astonished to see him, a teacher (rabbi), talking in public ' with a woman ' (John iv. 27, μετὰ γυναικὸς ἐλάλει).

(*d*) The ' pestle ' or ' mortar ' Pharisee. He walks with his head down in mock humility like a pestle in a mortar. He is also called the ' hump-backed ' Pharisee, who walked as though his shoulders bore the whole weight of the law, or the ' tumbling ' Pharisee, who was so humble that he would not lift his feet from the ground, or the ' painted ' Pharisee, who advertised his holiness by various poses, so that no one should touch and bring defilement to him. These are all caricatures, to be sure, of the true Pharisee, but they were so common that the Talmud [1] pictures them in great variety of detail—' the dyed ones who do evil deeds and claim godly recompense,' ' they who preach beautifully, but do not act beautifully.' Alexander Jannæus warned his wife against ' painted Pharisees who do the deeds of Zimri and look for the reward of Phinehas.' One is reminded of the charge of Jesus : ' For they say, and do not ' (Matt. xxiii. 3), of the broad phylacteries and the large borders on their garments, of the chief seats in the synagogues, and the salutations in the market places, and the wish to be hailed as Rabbi or Doctor (Matt. **xxiii**. 3-6).

(*e*) The ' ever-reckoning ' or ' compounding ' Pharisee.

---

[1] Jer. *Berachoth*, f. ix. 7, f. 13 ; Bab. *Sotah*, f. 22, 1 ; *Avoth d'Rabbi Nathan*, ch. 37.

He is always on the look-out for something 'extra' to do to make up for something that he has neglected. He is the 'reckon-it-up' Pharisee, trying to counterbalance his evil deeds with his good ones. He is anxious to have his few sins deducted from his many virtues and leave a clean balance-sheet. One is reminded of the Roman Catholic system for buying one out of purgatory and the whole system of indulgences. Pharisaism made a large contribution to Roman Catholic doctrine and life. It is easy to recall what Jesus said about tithing mint, dill, cummin, and about straining out gnats and swallowing camels.

(f) The 'timid' or 'fearing' Pharisee. His relation to God is that of trembling awe in dread of punishment. They imagine that they can satisfy God with outward performance, and keep the outside of the cup scrupulously clean, but neglect the inside of the cup (Luke xi. 39 f). They watch heaven with one eye and keep the other open for the main chance on earth, cross-eyed or cock-eyed instead of focussing both eyes in a single look at the glory of God (Matt. vi. 19-23). Hence, though ravening wolves, they will even put on sheep's clothing (Matt. vii. 15). This type of Pharisaism actually projected a conception of God as a devout Pharisee 'who repeats the Sh'ma to himself daily; wears phylacteries on the wrists and forehead; occupies Himself three times every day in studying His own law; has disputes with the angels about legal minutiæ; and finally summons a Rabbi to settle the difference.'[1]

(g) The 'God-loving' or 'born' Pharisee. This type is supposed to be like Abraham, and to show the true Pharisaism, of which the other six types are variations or perversions. Certainly, no one would say that all the Pharisees were hypocrites. Nor did Jesus mean that, but simply that hypocrisy had come to be the

[1] Farrar *Life of Lives*, p. 153.

distinguishing characteristic of Pharisees as a class or party. To this fact the Talmud itself bears clear testimony. The emphasis upon external observances drifted logically and naturally to that result. There were Pharisees who were friends of Jesus, men like Nicodemus, who cautiously felt their way and finally enlisted on his side. There were voluble Pharisees who quickly flocked to Christ, till he exposed their emptiness, when they deserted him (John viii. 30 f.).

7. *The Two Schools of Theology*

With all this variety among the Pharisees as pictured in the Talmud, it is no wonder that there were two schools of Pharisaism in Jerusalem (the school of Hillel and the school of Shammai) which took opposite positions on many points of theology, some of them trivial enough, as, for instance, whether it was proper to eat an egg laid by a hen on the Sabbath day. One is reminded of the Big Endians and the Little Endians in *Gulliver's Travels*. The Lilliputians split hopelessly on the grave issue as to which end to stand the egg upon. There was 'the plague of Pharisaism' in Palestine, and the Talmud bears its own terrible condemnation of it, in spite of its being the standard exposition of Pharisaic theology. It is urged by Buchler,[1] as we shall see later at more length, that it was the school of Shammai that made the washing of hands binding law about 100 A.D. against the protest of the school of Hillel. 'Up to this time the school of Shammai, and perhaps also some of the more strict Hillelites, may have practised the washing of hands ; but it was not yet binding law.' It was, he holds, insistence on strict Levitical purification for priests and teachers of the law that was the occasion of Christ's sharp criticism of the Shammai

[1] *Der Galiläische 'Am-ha-'arets des Zweiten Jahrhunderts*, pp. 127-131.

Pharisees in Mark vii. They championed the most narrow type of ceremonial piety and exclusiveness. Oesterley and Box [1] think that the school of Shammai was in the ascendant in Palestine up to A.D. 70, when the school of Hillel gained the upper hand. If so, this fact partially explains the intensity of Christ's denunciation of these rigorous legalists in such general terms. They were the real leaders of the majority. At the same time one is enabled to understand the friendly intercourse that existed between Christ and the Pharisees of the Hillel school of thought, who on occasion took his part against the school of Shammai. We see this division of sentiment among the Pharisees about Christ in John viii. 9, 16 ; x. 19-21 ; xii. 42. In Luke v. 17-26, the Pharisees are apparently greatly impressed by what Jesus said and did. So Chwolson [2] argues that Christ attacked only the extremists among the Pharisees, but he goes too far in exonerating the Pharisees from any part in the death of Jesus, and seeking to place all the blame on the Sadducees. Elbogen [3] reminds us that the Pharisees were the guardians of the Prophets and of the Hagiographa as well as of the Pentateuch.

8. *The Two Methods of Pharisaic Teaching*

In Ezra the Scribe it is common to find the origin of the Jewish scribes, and also of the Pharisees in principle, though not in time. We know not whether the 'assembly' described in Neh. x. became the great synagogue hypothecated by some scholars for this period. One of the treatises in the Mishna, called the *Pirké Aboth* or Sayings of the Fathers, ascribes this saying to the men of the Great Synagogue : ' Be deliberate in judgment ; make many disciples ; make a

[1] *Religion and Worship of the Synagogue*, p. 129.
[2] *Das letzte Passomahl Christi und der Tag des Todes*.
[3] *The Religious Views of the Pharisees*, p. 2.

THE PHARISAIC OUTLOOK

hedge for the law.' But no one knows who said this. Herford [1] regards this saying as the key to the interpretation of the Talmud : 'Deliberation in judgment is the key to the casuistry of the Talmud,' and thus even Herford admits the 'casuistry,' though he justifies it. It has always been the aim of Rabbinical Judaism to make disciples, and the hedge about the Torah was 'the means taken to keep the divine revelation from harm.' This saying does let us into the heart of the secret of Pharisaism. Herford [2] holds that, even apart from this saying, with the conception of the law held by Ezra, 'Pharisaism was certain to appear sooner or later, and the Talmud itself was the implied, though distant, result of the process by which that conception was to be worked out.' In other words, Herford maintains that Pharisaism is the natural and inevitable outcome of the Old Testament teaching, while Jesus made a distinct departure from the real Judaism of the past. This view misinterprets the Old Testament, the Pharisees and Jesus, in my opinion. At any rate, there is no doubt of the fact that Pharisaism grew out of the effort to honour the Torah, and was the religion of the Torah. But surely Herford [3] is asking too much when he asks us to feel sympathy with the idea that 'Rabbinical devotion could express itself quite naturally in terms which to the unenlightened Gentile appear extravagant —as, for instance, when it is said that God studies Torah for three hours every day' (b. A. Zar. 3b). He adds : [4] 'It is near the truth to say that what Christ is to the Christian, Torah is to the Jew.' With the Pharisees, Torah included the unwritten as well as the written word of God. Herford [5] unwittingly justifies Jesus when he says : 'And he (the Pharisee) would say that

---

[1] *Pharisaism*, p. 25. See also Taylor, *Sayings of the Jewish Fathers* (1897) ; Mielziner, *Introduction to the Talmud* (1903).
[2] *Pharisaism*, p. 28.   [3] *Ibid.*, p. 58.
[4] *Ibid.*, p. 171.   [5] *Ibid.*, p. 94.

the unwritten was more important than the written, because the unwritten unfolded what was concealed in the written, and extended its application.' This conception of the superiority of the oral law to the written on the part of the Pharisees is implied in what Josephus [1] says about their following the conduct of reason. Only they did not put it that way. This oral teaching or tradition of the elders was held to be authoritative. Rabbi Eleazar of Modin says: 'Whosoever interprets Scripture in opposition to tradition has no part in the future world.' Once more we read: 'The voice of the Rabbi is as the voice of God' (*Erubin*, fol. 21, col. 2), and 'To be against the word of the scribes is more punishable than to be against the word of the Bible' (*Sanh.* xi. 3). Surely Jesus [2] does not strain the point at all when he says with fine irony: 'Full well do ye reject the commandment of God that ye may keep your tradition.' In time the rabbis [3] came to say this: 'Moses received the (oral) Law from Sinai, and delivered it to Joshua and Joshua to the elders, and the elders to the prophets, and the prophets to the men of the great synagogue.' They either read all the oral law into the written law (eisegesis) or twisted it out of the written law (exegesis) in ways wonderful to behold.

The oral teaching itself (like the later Talmud) came to be divided into two parts (*Halachah* and *Haggadah*). In broad general terms *Halachah* (from הָלַךְ to go) means the way to go or rules of life, the rule of right conduct. This was the part that was considered binding and as authoritative as the Pentateuch itself. Much of it covered what is usually included by us in civil and criminal law. The rabbis were masters of canon and civil law, real LL.D.'s; or rather it was all one and the same with them. Lawyers and doctors of divinity were these rabbis, as we see them in the New Testa-

[1] *Ant.*, bk. xviii. ch. i. § 3.   [2] Mark vii. 9.   [3] *Pirkê Aboth*.

THE PHARISAIC OUTLOOK

ment. The *Halachah* included careful decisions arrived at with great deliberation, 'guided by the recorded opinion of earlier teachers, when known, and also by recognised rules of interpretation.'[1] The whole of life came under the control of the *Halachah*, as we shall see later. The *Halachah* is the most distinctive element in Pharisaic teaching, and received the most careful consideration.[2] By it they must in all fairness be judged. And yet Herford[3] says : ' It is the *Halachah* which has laid the Pharisees open to so much misrepresentation and obloquy.' One may properly ask if it is misrepresentation even if it is obloquy. ' Undoubtedly the rabbis thought that the *Halachah* as interpreted by them was the will of God. Hence they gave to that *Halachah*, which more than anything else has brought scorn and ridicule upon them, the patient labour of about six centuries.'[4] One example of the *Halachah* may be given. In Num. xv. 38 we read this command to Moses : ' Speak unto the children of Israel, and bid them that they make them fringes in the borders of their garments throughout their generations, and that they put upon the fringes of each border a cord of blue : and it shall be unto you for a fringe, that ye may look upon it, and remember the commandments of Jehovah, and do them.' This is just the kind of precept in the law that delighted the rabbis, and gave free range for expansion. The white wool and the blue threads would make pretty ' symbols of innocence and heaven.'[5] But the scribes ' added a mountainous mass of oral pedantries.'[6] They argued that the fringe must consist of four threads of white wool, one of which must be wound round the others as follows : seven times with a double knot, then eight times with a double knot, then eleven times with

---

[1] Herford, *Pharisaism*, p. 97. [2] *Ibid.*, p. 96. [3] *Ibid.*
[4] *Ibid.*, p. 108.
[5] Farrar, *Life of Lives*, p. 157. [6] *Ibid.*

a double knot, then thirteen times with a double knot, 'because 7+8+11=26, the numerical value of the letters of Jehovah (יהוה), and 13 is the numerical value of *Achad*, one, so that the number of windings represents the words "Jehovah is one."'[1] But what shall we say to the remark of Rashi (Rabbi Solomon Isaaki, 1040-1105 A.D.), 'the prince of commentators' on the Talmud? He says: 'The precept concerning the fringes is as weighty as all the other precepts put together,' and again he says: 'He who observes the precept about the fringes shall have 2800 slaves to wait on him.'[2] Of this custom Jesus said: 'They enlarge the borders' or fringes of their garments (μεγαλύνουσιν κράσπεδα) for purposes of display, with all the Pharisaic knots tied according to the rules of the rabbis in the *Halachah*. By *Halachah*, therefore, the Pharisees meant all the legal and ritual element in the Scripture, and all 'the usages, customs (*Minhāgîm*), ordinances (*Teqanôth*) and decrees (*Gezērôth*) for which there is little or no authority in the Scripture.'[3]

But what is the *Haggadah*? This term is from *nagad* (נגד), to say, and was applied to all the interpretations of Scripture that were not precept.[4] Under this designation we find almost anything about everything. The rabbis by no means agreed with themselves, and they did not require uniformity of belief in every detail. A rabbi could say utterly contradictory things if it was merely *Haggadah*, for it was not binding. Weber[5] is justly open to criticism, for seeking to produce a system of Pharisaic theology in so far forth as the *Haggadah* is concerned. Herford[6] sarcastically remarks: 'Chris-

[1] Farrar, *Life of Lives*, p. 158.
[2] *Shabbath*, f. 29, 1; *Maccoth*, f. 23, 2.
[3] Schechter, *Studies in Judaism*, p. 228.
[4] Bacher, *Jewish Quarterly Review*, 1892, pp. 406 ff.; cf. also Herford, *Pharisaism*, p. 232.
[5] *Jüdische Theologie auf Grund des Talmud, etc.*, 2 Aufl. 1897.
[6] *Pharisaism*, p. 236.

THE PHARISAIC OUTLOOK

tian scholars are pathetically grateful to Weber for having given them an orderly and methodical arrangement of the medley of Pharisaic doctrines; certainly he has done so, but with as much success and as much truth as if he had described a tropical jungle, believing it to be a nursery-garden.' Anything may find a place in the *Haggadah*, provided it can be shown to have some vague connection with a word or letter of Scripture, however irrelevant the interpretation, illustration, or application may be. Here we find 'astronomy and astrology, medicine and magic, theosophy and mysticism.'[1] In popular form the rabbis have had free play for imagination, for anecdote, for parable, for fable. Recall Paul's warnings to Timothy against 'fables and endless genealogies' (1 Tim. i. 4), 'profane and old wives' fables' (iv. 7), and to Titus against those who give heed to 'Jewish fables and commandments of men' (i. 14).

Hear Herford[2] again, the modern apologist of Pharisaism: 'Ethical principles, mystical speculations, meditations on providence and the wonders of creation, the imaginings of pious fantasy, and even the play of daring wit. No freak of allegory, of word-play, of fantastic juggling with letters and syllables, is without illustration in the *Haggadah*.' The *Haggadah* dealt with what a man was to believe and to feel (his theology), while the *Halachah* set forth what he was to do (morality or ethics).[3] *Halachah* led to pure externalism, 'all that was internal and higher being merely *Haggadic*,'[4] and so not binding. This distinction drove a wedge between the spiritual and intellectual on one side, and the performance of rites and ceremonies as real religion on the other. As a specimen of *Halachah* we read

---

[1] Schechter, *Studies in Judaism*, p. 228.
[2] *Pharisaism*, p. 241.
[3] Edersheim, *Life and Times of Jesus the Messiah*, vol. i. p. 106.
[4] *Ibid.*, p. 106.

(B. *Meg.* 86d) that during a discussion about purity in the heavenly academy Rabbah was summoned from earth to prove the correctness of the Almighty's opinion on the subject. Once more the Talmud tells us how to see demons. Rabbi [1] says: 'Whoever wishes to see them let him take the interior covering of a black cat, the kitten of a first-born black cat, which is also the kitten of a first-born, and let him burn it in the fire, and powder it, and fill his eyes with it, and he will see them.'

It must be borne in mind that the distinction between *Halachah* and *Haggadah* applies both to the Midrash [2] and the Talmud.[3] The Mishna was mainly *Halachah*, but the Gemara was largely *Haggadah*. The Babylonian Talmud, which is the one in common use among Jews to-day, is more casuistical in the Gemara than the Palestinian.[4] 'It was said by some that the written law was like water, the Mishnah like wine, and the Gemara like *hippocras* or spiced wine.' [5] The Babylonian Gemara had an extra touch of spice.

I cannot pose as an impartial witness, but I have never read a book so dull as the minutiæ and hair-splitting tortuosities of the Mishna and the Gemara. One opens almost anywhere and it requires a positive effort to go on. This wine has lost its flavour for me. Take this specimen, selected at random (*Baba Kamma*, ch. iv. Mishna iii.). Mishna: 'An ox belonging to an Israelite that gored an ox belonging to the sanctuary, or of the sanctuary that gored one of a commoner, there is no liability, for it is written: the ox of another but not of the sanctuary, Ex. xxi. xxxi.' Gemara: 'This Mishna is not in accordance with R. Simeon b. Menassia of the following Boraitha: An ox of a commoner that

[1] *Berachoth*, fol. 6, col. 1.
[2] See Oesterley, *Religion and Worship of the Synagogue*, pp. 79-95.
[3] *Ibid.*, pp. 55-68.   [4] *Ibid.*, p. 69.
[5] Pick, *The Talmud*, p. 69.

gored an ox of the sanctuary ; or *vice versa*, is free, for it is written, an ox of another, but not of the sanctuary. R. Simeon b. Menassia, however, says that an ox of the sanctuary that gored an ox of a commoner is free, but an ox of a commoner that gored an ox of the sanctuary, whether vicious or not, the whole damage must be paid.' And on the twistification and casuistry go for another page.

It is not possible to give a picture of the long line of rabbis who have given themselves so devotedly to the explication of the involutions of the Torah. The Talmud and the Midrash are the chief monuments of their wisdom and their industry. Each rabbi sought to add one great saying to the endless store to be passed on to future generations. Hillel's great rule was: 'That which is hateful to thyself do not do to thy neighbour. This is the whole law, and the rest is mere commentary'[1] —the negative form of the Golden Rule. The great word of his rival Shammai was : ' Let thy repetition of the law be at a fixed hour ; speak little, but do that which thou hast to do with cheerful countenance.'[2] The word of Gamaliel I., Rabban, 'Our Teacher,' the teacher of the Apostle Paul, was : ' Procure thyself a teacher, avoid being in doubt, and do not accustom thyself to give tithes by guess.'[3] Gamaliel had gained some knowledge of Greek literature, a heresy from the standpoint of the rabbis, but he was excused on the ground that he needed it for diplomatic intercourse with the government.

9. *The Chief Points in Pharisaic Theology*

At once we are confronted with the importance and the difficulty of distinguishing between the later theology

[1] *Shabbath*, fol. 31, col. 1.
[2] *Aboth*, i. 15.   [3] *Ibid.*, i. 16.

of the rabbis and that current in Palestine, in the first century A.D. Clearly both *Halachah* and *Haggadah* are far more extensive in the written Midrash than was true in the time of Jesus. But Herford [1] admits that 'the intention of it is the same for the earlier as for the later. Wherefore it is legitimate to use the Talmud, to illustrate the principle of *Halachah*, as accepted in the New Testament period.' But, as already stated, the theology of the Pharisees, so far as their beliefs were concerned, was mainly *Haggadah*. But the New Testament, Josephus, the Psalms of Solomon, the Testaments of the Twelve Patriarchs, 2 Esdras, the Talmud, and the Midrash agree in the main outlines of Pharisaic theology. We can only give the picture in bold outline.

Elbogen [2] is right in his plea that justice be done the Pharisees, for the preservation of monotheism in opposition to the powerful pressure of Greek polytheism, for the emphasis on individualism, and for the prominence of belief in a future life. It is impossible to over-estimate the value placed upon the study of Torah by the rabbis. Rabbi Jacob said (*Pirké Aboth*, iii. 10) : 'He who is walking by the way and studying, and breaks off his Mishnah (study) and says, How fine is this tree! and how fine is this fallow! they account it to him as if he were guilty of death.' Again Rabbi Dosithai says (iii. 12) in the name of Rabbi Meir : 'When a scholar of the wise sits and studies and has forgotten a word of his Mishnah, they account it unto him as if he were guilty of death.' Once more Rabbi Li'eser (*Pirké Aboth*, ii. 14) says : 'Warm thyself before the fire of the wise, but beware of their embers, perchance thou mayest be singed, for their bite is the bite of a fox, and their sting the sting of a scorpion, and their hiss the hiss of a fiery serpent, and all their words are as coals of fire.'

[1] *Pharisaism*, p. 249.
[2] *The Religious Views of the Pharisees*, p. 2.

Rabban Jochanan ben Zakai placed such an estimate upon one of his disciples, that he said (*Pirké Aboth*, ii. 2) : 'If all the wise of Israel were in a scale of a balance, and Eli'ezer ben Hyrqanos in the other scale, he would outweigh them all.'

In a way the Pharisees as a whole were theological moderates as between Sadducees and Hellenisers on the one hand, and the Essenes on the other. The Essenes were far more reactionary than the Pharisees, while the Sadducees lent a listening ear to the allurements of Hellenism. The outstanding features of Pharisaic theology, as distinct from practice, are easily grasped. They are four.

(a) They held both to divine sovereignty and human free agency. The Essenes were fatalists and denied human responsibility, while the Sadducees rejected divine sovereignty over man's actions. Josephus speaks of the matter twice. In *Antiquities*, bk. xviii. ch. i. § 3, he says : 'When they determine that all things are done by fate, they do not take away the freedom from men of acting as they think fit ; since their notion is that it hath pleased God to make a temperament, whereby what He wills is done, but so that the will of man can act virtuously or viciously.' Josephus here occupies the standpoint and uses the language of Greek philosophy, but properly represents the Pharisees on this point as the Talmud shows. In the *War*, bk. ii. ch. viii. § 14, he says : 'These ascribe all to fate and to God, yet they allow, that to act what is right, or the contrary, is principally in the power of man, although fate does co-operate in every action.' By 'fate' Josephus means the personal God, not a mere abstraction like the view of the Stoics. On this point, which is fundamental, the Pharisees occupied in general the standpoint about God and man that modern Calvinists maintain.

(b) They placed the oral law on a par with the Old Testament Scriptures. We have had this point illustrated already, but let us bear in mind Josephus again. In *Antiquities*, bk. xiii. ch. x. § 6, he says : 'What I would now explain is this, that the Pharisees have delivered to the people a great many observances by succession from their fathers, which are not written in the laws of Moses ; and for that reason it is that the Sadducees reject them, and say that we are to esteem those observances to be obligatory which are in the written word, but are not to observe what are delivered from the tradition of our forefathers.' Josephus wrote in the latter part of the first century A.D., but long before any of the oral law was written down in Mishna or Gemara. Josephus pays this tribute to Pharisaic exegesis : 'The Pharisees are those who are esteemed most skilful in the exact explanation of their laws' (*War*, bk. ii. ch. viii. § 14). And this also : 'They also pay a respect to such as are in years ; nor are they so bold as to contradict them in anything which they have introduced.' That is more euphemistic, at any rate, than the language of Jesus : 'They bind heavy burdens and grievous to be borne, and lay them on men's shoulders ; but they themselves will not move them with their finger' (Matt. xxiii. 4). Hear now some of the Jewish Fathers on the subject of learning this oral law : 'There are four characters in scholars. Quick to hear and quick to forget, his gain is excelled by his loss ; slow to hear and slow to forget, his loss is excelled by his gain ; quick to hear and slow to forget, is wise : slow to hear and quick to forget, this is an evil lot' (*Pirké Aboth*, v. 18). These correspond somewhat to the four temperaments. And then this : 'There are four characters in college-goers. He that goes and does not practise, the reward of going is in his hand : he that practises and does not go, the reward of practice

THE PHARISAIC OUTLOOK

is in his hand : he that practises is pious : he that goes not and does not practise is wicked ' (v. 20). And once more this : ' At five years old, Scripture : at ten years, Mishna : at thirteen, the Commandments : at fifteen, Talmud : at eighteen, the bridal : at twenty, pursuits : at thirty, strength : at forty, discernment : at fifty, counsel : at sixty, age : at seventy, hoariness : at eighty, power : at ninety, decrepitude : at a hundred, it is as though he were dead, and gone and had ceased from the world.'

(c) The Pharisees believed in the future life. The Sadducees scouted this idea and the absence of any definite teaching on the subject in the Pentateuch. And yet Jesus refuted the Sadducees on this very point with a quotation from the Pentateuch, and charged them with ignorance of the Scriptures and of the power of God when they failed to see that God, as the God of Abraham and Isaac and Jacob, is the God of the living and not of the dead.[1] On this subject Josephus says of the Pharisees : ' They also believe that souls have an immortal vigour in them, and that under the earth there will be rewards or punishments, according as they have lived virtuously or viciously in this life ; and the latter are to be detained in an everlasting prison, but that the former shall have power to revive and live again.' [2] Josephus also [3] puts it thus : ' They say that all souls are incorruptible, but that the souls of good men only are removed into other bodies, but that the souls of bad men are subject to eternal punishment.' It is interesting to note that the words of Josephus about ' eternal punishment ' are quite similar to those used by Jesus [4] in Matt. xxv. 46. But we must not argue that the Pharisees held to the transmigration of

---

[1] Matt. xxii. 29-33 ; Mark xii. 24-27 ; Luke xx. 34-40.
[2] *Ant.*, bk. xviii. ch. i. § 3.   [3] *War*, bk. ii. ch. viii. § 14.
[4] Josephus has ἀΐδια τιμωρία κολάσεσθαι while Jesus is reported as using εἰς κόλασιν αἰώνιον.

souls. The language of Josephus is probably due to his effort to put doctrine in a way not to shock Hellenic ideas, since the Greek contempt for the body made the idea of the resurrection of the body abhorrent to both Greeks and Romans.[1] In this matter the Pharisees follow the main lines of Jewish doctrine (cf. Dan. xii. 2). In the Psalms of Solomon, only the resurrection of the righteous is presented :[2] 'The life of the righteous is for ever. But sinners shall be taken away unto destruction.' Again : 'But they that fear the Lord shall rise again unto life eternal' (Ps. of Sol. iii. 16). Hence in the New Testament the Pharisees are represented as believing in angels and spirits, which the Sadducees deny (Acts xxiii. 8).

(*d*) The Pharisees had messianic expectations. It is not easy to present in one paragraph the conceptions of the Messiah held by the Pharisees. But at least it can be said at once that they revived and preserved belief in the Messiah, however mistaken their idea of Him was. The Sadducees expected no Messiah. The Apocrypha has a strange dearth of reference to the Messiah. The oppressions of Antiochus Epiphanes quickened faith in the future life and in the Messiah as the Deliverer of Israel. Curiously enough, Josephus, though himself a Pharisee of the liberal sort (somewhat like the modern reformed Jews), does not mention the Messiah as the belief of the Pharisees in his description of them. He does, indeed, give one paragraph (*Ant.*, bk. xviii. ch. iii. § 3) in which he describes Jesus as one who was 'Christ,' which term he probably used more as a proper name or as an appellative in the language of the people, without admitting that Jesus was really the Messiah of Jewish hopes. It is possible to take the passage as it stands in this sense

---

[1] Thomson, *Intern. Stand. Bible Encycl.*   [2] xiii. 9 f.

(so Burkitt and Harnack)[1] without having to eliminate it (all or part) as Christian addition. Josephus's own belief on the subject of the Messiah appears in *War*, bk. vi. ch. v. § 4, where he refers to 'an ambiguous oracle in their sacred writings' which had deceived many of their wise men into thinking that the Messiah belonged to the Jews alone. Josephus pointedly says: 'Now this oracle denoted the government of Vespasian who was appointed emperor in Judea.' Crude as this view appears, one must remember that Josephus wrote after the destruction of Jerusalem and the Jewish temple, and after the Jewish state had disappeared. And in the reign of Hadrian about a hundred years after the death of Jesus, it was the great Rabbi Aqiba who led the revolt against Hadrian, in order to establish Bar-Cochba (son of a star) as the political Messiah. The Pharisees rejected Jesus as the Messiah, and the great Pharisaic leader a hundred years later accepted Bar-Cochba as Messiah. But it was a political Messiah that the Pharisees expected, and in that sense they received Bar-Cochba with such lamentable results. There is ground for thinking that, if Jesus had been willing to pose as a political Messiah, with the claim of a world kingdom to throw off the Roman yoke, the Pharisees would have rallied round him. Indeed, on one occasion, there was a popular uprising to take Jesus by force and make Him king, since the crowd was persuaded that He was the prophet that was to come into the world (John vi. 14 f.). The Pharisees did not agree in all their ideas about this Messiah, but in broad outline they did. The political kingdom was to be presided over by the king Messiah, who was not divine, and yet was supernatural in mission and in manifestation.[2] He is pre-mundane, and possibly eternal in His

---

[1] See also Seitz, *Christus-Zeugnisse aus dem klassischen Altertum*, 1896, pp. 9 ff.   [2] Syb. Oracles, vv. 285 f.; Enoch, xlvii. 3.

pre-existence.[1] He is the Son of Man [2] and the Son of God,[3] though we have to use Enoch with great caution, because of the uncertainty as to the dates of the various portions. In the Psalms of Solomon the Messiah is free from sin,[4] the Son of David to reign over Israel, the righteous king, taught of God, Christ the Lord.[5] Here (Psalms of Solomon xvii. 23-30) we see the popular expectations of the Messiah. In the Talmud many marvels are presented that were to accompany the coming of the Messiah, which was to be sudden.[6] Some thought that the Messiah was to come with apocalyptic display out of heaven. Thus is to be understood the frequent request of the Pharisees for Jesus to produce a sign from heaven. The devil apparently had this idea in mind when he suggested to Jesus to let the people see Him sailing down from the pinnacle of the temple. So the rabble in Jerusalem argue: 'Howbeit, we know this man whence he is: but when Christ cometh no one knoweth whence he is' (John vii. 27). Little effort was made to combine into a coherent whole these contradictory views of a human and yet a supernatural Messiah (Stanton, *The Jewish and the Christian Messiah*, 1886, pp. 135 f.). But there seems to be no connection with Philo's *logos* teaching (Baldensperger, *Selbstbewusstsein Jesu*, p. 88).

The Pharisees did not expect a suffering or dying Messiah.[7] They would hear nothing of a Messiah that was not to set up His political kingdom and throw off the Roman yoke, but who was simply to die and pass away. They wanted one who would abide for ever (John xii. 34). But we cannot close this discussion

---

[1] Cf. Targum on Isa. ix. 6; Micah v. 2.
[2] Enoch xlviii. 2.   [3] Enoch cv. 2.   [4] xvii. 41.
[5] xvii. 35 f. Here the LXX translation of Lam. iv. 20 occurs (Χριστὸς Κύριος) as we have it in Luke ii. 11.
[6] Cf. Edersheim, *Life and Times*, vol. i. pp. 176 f.
[7] Dalman, *Der leidende und sterbende Messias*, 1888, pp. 3, 22 f.

THE PHARISAIC OUTLOOK

without a word about the identification of the Messianic hope with John Hyrcanus I., who was regarded as prophet, priest, and king, thus abandoning the tribe of Judah for the tribe of Levi. This transition appears in the *Book of Jubilees* and in the *Testaments of the Twelve Patriarchs*. Charles[1] makes a clear statement of this phase of the subject. See *Test. Levi*, viii. 14 : 'A king shall arise in Judah, and shall establish a new priesthood. . . . And his presence is beloved as a prophet of the Most High.' This was applied to John Hyrcanus I. in the height of Pharisaic enthusiasm, but alas! for human hopes, John Hyrcanus deserted the Pharisees for the Sadducees, and therewith perished this Messianic hope. But the two nerve centres of Judaism were the love of the law and the hope of the Messiah. The two poles round which Jewish life revolved were 'fulfilment of the law and hope of future glory.'[2] The temple and the synagogue kept up the fulfilment of the law and of tradition under the tutelage of priest and scribe. The hope of the future fell in the main to the apocalyptists,[3] who must have separate treatment directly   We are not quite done with the work of the scribe.

10. *The Practice of Pharisaism in Life*

Let us quote Herford again. 'Paul condemned Pharisaism in theory, while Jesus condemned it in practice.'[4] Jesus 'was really rejected, so far at all events as the Pharisees were concerned, because He undermined the authority of the Torah, and endangered the religion founded upon it.'[5] Once more hear Herford : 'Torah and Jesus could not remain in har-

---

[1] *Religious Development between the Old and the New Testaments*, pp. 79-84.
[2] Schuerer, *Jewish People*, div. ii. vol. ii. p. 93.
[3] Herford, *Pharisaism*, p. 191.   [4] *Ibid.*, p. 143.   [5] *Ibid.*, p. 146.

mony. The two were fundamentally incompatible.' We must therefore see what is the Pharisaic view of life that clashed so sharply with that of Jesus. We may note at once that it is *Halachah*, not *Haggadah*, with which we are now concerned. These matters are binding. 'It is more culpable to teach contrary to the precepts of the scribes than contrary to the Torah itself.' [1] These precepts for conduct applied to every detail of life. Nothing is left to chance, or to the initiative or conscience of the individual. Everything is worked out with casuistical hypothesis, and it is all important and necessary. 'There is no real distinction of great and small, important and trivial, in the things that are done in accordance with *Halachah*,' says Herford.[2] So Josephus : [3] 'Now, for the Pharisees, they live meanly, and despise delicacies in diet. . . . And whatsoever they (the people) do about Divine worship, prayers, and sacrifices, they perform them according to their direction.'

The Pharisees applied their interpretation of the ceremonial law to the Sabbath, to meals, to ablutions, to travel, to trade, to dealings with Gentiles, to relations with the '*Am-ha-'arets*, to tithing, to everything. All this led to that externalism and professionalism in religious service that Jesus condemned so severely. But we must hear the Pharisees themselves. Twelve treatises of the Mishna discuss the subject of purification. 'He who lightly esteems hand-washing will perish from the earth' (*Sotah*, iv.). The rabbis found forty-nine reasons for pronouncing each animal clean or unclean, and pronounced seven hundred kinds of fish and twenty-four kinds of birds unclean.[4] Imagine therefore the terror of Simon Peter, in his vision on the house-top at Joppa, when he was invited by the Lord to rise, slay

---

[1] *Sanhedrin*, xi. 3.
[2] *Pharisaism*, p. 101
[3] *Ant.*, bk. xviii. ch. i. § 3.
[4] *Sopherim*, xvi. 6.

THE PHARISAIC OUTLOOK

and eat all manner of beasts and birds, and he a pious Jew. The rabbis added many regulations about the observance of mere rules, and then found them so inconvenient that they devised plans for evading them, for they were lawyers and fulfilled one of the functions of the modern lawyer in showing one's clients how to evade the law. The *Book of Jubilees* [1] has this paragraph about the Sabbath: 'Every one who desecrates the Sabbath, or declares that he intends to make a journey on it, or speaks either of buying or selling, or he who draws water and has not provided it upon the sixth day, and he who lifts a burden in order to take it out of his dwelling-place, or out of his house shall die. And every one who makes a journey, or attends to his cattle, and he who kindles a fire, or rides upon any beast, or sails upon a ship on the sea upon the Sabbath day, shall die.' Hear the Talmud: 'A fracture may not be attended to. If any one has sprained his hand or foot, he may not pour cold water on it.' [2] One was not allowed to write on the Sabbath, save on something dark or with the hand upside down. One is not allowed to read by lamplight or to cleanse clothing. Women were not to look in the mirror on the Sabbath day because they might see a grey hair and be tempted to pull it out. Some knots could be tied on the Sabbath and others not. One must state what kind of a knot it was. To untie the knot of camel drivers and of sailors is a sin, while a knot that can be untied with one hand is allowed. One must not kindle a fire on the Sabbath. Some churches in America used to consider it a sin to have fire in church on Sunday. Vinegar could be used for sore throat if it was swallowed, but not as a gargle. If the burden grew too heavy, one could evade these heavy laws by the rule of intention. An egg laid on the Sabbath day could be eaten, provided one intended to kill

[1] 50.   [2] *Shabbath*, xxii. 6.

the hen.[1] So an ox[2] could be taken out of the ditch if one intended to kill it. In case of peril of life, one was allowed to send for the physician. The Jews, after the unfortunate experience of Mattathias, would fight on the Sabbath, but only in the case of attack by the enemy.[3]

But 'life under the law' had the added burden of the distinction between the clean and the unclean. This applied to persons and things and places. Part of these rules rested on the Levitical laws, and have a basis of value for hygienic purposes, and so as a means of keeping the people of Israel separate from the idolatrous practices of the Gentiles. But the rabbis could not rest content with the details of the law of Moses. They must define the most minute items with no chance of mistake. In the matter of utensils there was the question of material (earthen, wooden, leathern, glass, iron, gold, silver) and the shape (whether hollow or flat). If the vessel is unclean and one's hands are clean, how shall he take hold of the vessel ? If the vessel is broken, what is to be done ? Then the problem of purification is a serious one. There is pond water, spring water, running water in streams, collected water from the pond or spring or stream or rain water, and clean water and unclean water. Each kind has its special function, and must be properly used if one is to be clean.[4] If rain water and river water are mixed in the bath, what is one to do ? And then what about hail, snow, frost, and dew ? And then the hands must be washed before eating. Pouring water on the hands would answer for ordinary purposes, but in case of eating holy things the hands must be completely dipped

---

[1] On the whole subject of the Sabbath, see Schuerer, *Jewish People*, div. ii. vol. ii. pp. 96-105.
[2] These examples come from the Tractate *Shabbath* in the Mishna.
[3] Josephus, *Ant.*, bk. xiv. ch. iv. § 2.
[4] See the Tractate *Kelim*.

THE PHARISAIC OUTLOOK

in water. The cups, platters, pots must be properly cleansed. Piety came at a high price to the Pharisees.

And then one must be careful about his associates. Were they clean? The Jews had no dealings with the Samaritans, and kept away from the homes of Gentiles. Peter's apology to Cornelius (Acts x. 28) for violating the law of his people by entering his house is a case in point. A rabbi must not talk with a woman in public and not too much with his wife, else he will go to Gehenna. In the Jewish Prayer Book [1] we read: 'Blessed art thou, O Lord God, King of the universe, who hast not made me a heathen. Blessed art thou . . . who hast not made me a bondman. Blessed art thou . . . who hast not made me a woman.' The Pharisee thus has pride of race, of position, of sex, and of laborious personal purity by attention to the formulæ for righteousness, by doing which he gained salvation. In all this he thought that he was doing the will of God. Rabbi ben Tema [2] says: 'Be bold as a leopard, light as an eagle, swift as a stag, and strong as a lion, to do the will of your Father in heaven.' It is easy to see that the study of these details required time. In Sirach xxxviii. 24-26 we read:

'The wisdom of a scribe cometh by opportunity of leisure;
And he that hath little business shall become wise.
How can he get wisdom that holdeth the plow,
That glorieth in the goad,
That driveth oxen, and is occupied in their labours,
And whose talk is of bullocks?'

Here is fine scorn for 'clodhoppers' or the '*Am-ha-'arets*, the people of the land. Josephus [3] had a sort of contempt for this casuistry, as we see: 'For there was a certain sect of men that were Jews, who valued themselves highly upon the exact skill they had in the law

---
[1] Singer, Auth. Ed., p. 5. [2] *Pirké Aboth*, v. 20.
[3] *Ant.*, bk. xvii. ch. ii. § 4.

of their fathers, and made men believe they were highly favoured by God, by whom this set of women was inveigled. . . . A cunning sect they were.' But with all these peccadillos, and partly by reason of them, the Pharisees had the multitude on their side,[1] while the Sadducees were able to persuade none but the rich.

11. *The Apocalyptists*

It is good to turn to a more pleasing phase of Jewish life and thought, even if only for a moment. The apocalyptists took the place of the prophets, and grew up beside the scribes. In the main they seem to have been Pharisees, though they did not belong to the main stream of Pharisaic thought.[2] Certain aspects of their teaching were incorporated by the Pharisees, as in their Messianic expectations presented in the Sybilline Oracles, Book of Enoch, Psalms of Solomon, and 2 Esdras. Apocalypse was resorted to as a means of expressing the hopes of the people in times of persecution. We see it in Ezekiel, Daniel, and Zechariah. The persecutions under Antiochus Epiphanes stimulated it. They were often pseudepigraphic, with the idea that the name of an ancient worthy would gain a hearing for their message. The veiled form of the message in symbols made it a pillar of light for the initiated, and a cloud of darkness for the enemies of the chosen people. The apocalyptists deal mainly with the future hopes of the people. They kept alive the fire when it was hard to do it. Charles (*Religious Devel.*, p. 45) says : ' All Jewish apocalypses, therefore, from 200 B.C. onwards, were of necessity pseudonymous if they sought to exercise any real influence on the nation ; for the Law was everything, belief in inspiration was dead amongst them, and the canon was closed.' It is

---

[1] Josephus, *Ant.*, bk. xiii. ch. x. § 6.

[2] Thomson, however, thinks (art. 'Apocalyptical Literature' in *Inter. Stand. Bible Encycl.*) that most of these books were written by Essenes.

clear that eschatological elements in the teaching exist. I am not able to follow Schweitzer, and make that the determining factor in the message of Jesus. That is to me a very one-sided view of the facts. Indeed, the positive ethical note (not mere *interim* ethics) is present in the Jewish apocalyptists along with the confused eschatology. Both John the Baptist and Jesus made use of the apocalyptic imagery of the Old Testament and of the popular writers of later days. These apocalyptists were largely neglected by the rabbinical legalists, but their ideas had gained a powerful hold on certain elements of the people. The law stood in the way of fresh truth, and the apocalyptists had no easy task. Indeed, the best of these books, the Testaments of the Twelve Patriarchs, ' was never officially accepted or otherwise by the Pharisees. It was never authoritative save in certain circles of Pharisaic mystics, who must in due time have found a congenial home in the bosom of the rising Christian Church. So little did the Pharisaic legalists—the dominating power of Pharisaism—appreciate this work that they did not think it worth preserving. For its preservation the world is indebted to the Christian church.'[1] In fact, it is by no means clear whether the book, as we now have it, has not been largely interpolated by Christian writers who have inserted teachings of Jesus here and there. At any rate, the teaching in this book is not sacramental legalism, but is a much nearer approach to that of Jesus in its emphasis upon the inward and the spiritual. Charles[2] shows

---

[1] Charles, *Rel. Devel.*, p. 157.
[2] *Ibid.*, pp. 151 ff. See further Burkitt, *Jewish and Christian Apocalypses*; Cook, *The Fathers of Jesus*; Thomson, *Books which have Influenced Our Lord*; Danziger, *Jewish Forerunners of Jesus*; Toy, *Judaism and Christianity*; Hughes, *Ethics of Jewish Apocryphal Literature*; Schweitzer, *The Quest of the Historical Jesus*; Sanday, *The Life of Christ in Recent Research*; Dobschütz, *Eschatology of the Gospels*; Worsley, *The Apocalypse of Jesus*; Winstanley, *Jesus and the Future*; Dewick, *Primitive Christian Eschatology*; Kennedy, *St. Paul's Conceptions of Last Things*.

that the teaching of the Testaments concerning forgiveness of injuries is far superior to that in the Talmud, and 'is in keeping with the entire ethical character of that remarkable book, which proclaims in an ethical setting that God created man in His own image, that the law was given to lighten every man, that salvation was for all mankind through conversion to Judaism, and that a man should love both God and his neighbour.' It is entirely possible that Zacharias and Elizabeth, Simeon and Anna, Joseph and Mary, John and Jesus knew the teachings of this side of Jewish thought, the apocalyptic tone and shading behind which glimmered the real flame in spiritual life. But the collision between the Pharisees and Jesus was in a different realm. The Pharisees themselves regarded the apocalyptists as an eddy in the stream. The real Pharisees we have seen as pictured in their own writings. What will they think of and do to the new Rabbi, who suddenly appears in the temple, and usurps authority in the home of priest and scribe?

They stand in Jerusalem entrenched in the hearts of the people as the exponents of current Jewish orthodoxy and professors of special holiness, the preservers of traditional Judaism. They sit in Moses' seat with all the authority of hoary antiquity. They stand against the tide of Hellenism and every theological upstart. No one can be an accredited teacher of Judaism without their *imprimatur*. They had trouble with John the Baptist. One day Jesus appears in the temple with a scourge of cords in His hands. He has asserted His Messianic authority over priest and scribe, Sadducee and Pharisee. The Pharisees have reached a crisis in their history. What shall they do with Jesus?

CHAPTER II

THE PHARISAIC RESENTMENT TOWARD JESUS

SINCE the Jews and apologists for Pharisaism complain that the Gospels and Paul's Epistles treat the Pharisees unfairly, it is only fair to begin with the Talmud to interpret Jewish feeling toward Jesus. Herford (*Christianity in Talmud and Midrash*, 1903, p. 7) insists that 'it is obvious that the Rabbinical literature must also be consulted, if a thorough investigation into the origin of Christianity is to be made.'

1. *The Spirit of the Talmud toward Jesus*

It is not necessary here to discuss at length the question whether the Talmud quotes the Gospels or the Gospels the Talmud. Renan [1] argued that it was inadmissible to assert that the compilers of the Talmud made any use of the Gospels or any Christian teaching. This idea of Renan was championed by Deutsch,[2] who alleged that to maintain that the Talmud made use of the New Testament would be like saying that Sanscrit sprang from Latin. The point in this argument is that the Talmud rests mainly on oral tradition that antedates the Gospels and the teachings of Jesus. But Wellhausen [3] brands this theory 'a mere superstition,' and holds that the Talmud 'is based on literature and

---

[1] *Life of Jesus*, p. 108.
[2] *The Quarterly Review*, Oct. 1867.
[3] *Israelitische und jüdische Geschichte*, 1894, p. 37 *footnote*.

refers to literature.'[1] Pick[2] shows that a number of these parallels in the Talmud to sayings of Jesus are referred 'to rabbis who lived a long time after Jesus.' He holds this view to be 'a vain glorification of modern Judaism, which, on the one hand, rejects the Talmud as a religious code, but makes use of it for controversial purposes.' Stapfer,[3] who once asserted that Hillel was the real forerunner and teacher of Jesus, renounced his former opinion as erroneous. Hillel is the only rabbi of importance whose sayings at all parallel those of Jesus, and who also lived before Christ. There are, beyond a doubt, excellent maxims, 'even some close parallels to the utterances of Christ' (Farrar, *Life of Christ*, vol. ii. p. 485), but they are chiefly proverbs more or less common to the age. And in these parallels the saying of Jesus has a crispness and originality all its own. Take for instance this, the most famous of all, the so-called Golden Rule, which in one form or another is used by Isocrates, Diogenes Laertius (from Aristotle), Confucius, Tobit, the Epistle of Aristeas, Hillel. The form of Hillel is this : 'What is hateful to thee, do not to another. This is the whole law, all else is only commentary.' Jesus says : 'Therefore all things whatsoever ye would that men should do to you, do ye even so to them ; for this is the law and the prophets.' It is possible that in some instances the Talmud made use of Christian teaching, since it did incorporate matter from neighbours of the Babylonian Jews, and from others more or less hostile to the Jews.[4]

One has to call attention also to the fact that the Talmud as now published is much less severe toward Jesus than was once the case. Farrar[5] notes that the

---

[1] Translation of B. Pick, *Jesus in the Talmud*, p. 75.
[2] *Ibid.*, 1913, p. 78.
[3] *Palestine in the Time of Christ*, 3rd ed., p. 289.
[4] Dunlap Moore, *Talmud in Schaff-Herzog Encyclopedia*.
[5] *Life of Christ*, vol. ii. p. 452.

name of Jesus appears only about twenty times in unexpurgated editions of the Talmud, the last of which was published in Amsterdam in 1644. Professor B. Pick [1] has one of these collections of the Talmudic sayings about Jesus, which was published in 1644 by the Jews themselves, for the benefit of other Jews after the Jewish Synod at Petrikau, Poland (A.D. 1631), issued a circular to the effect that future editions of the Talmud should omit the passages about Jesus. Other copies of the collection exist also. Dalman has published this collection of the passages expurgated from the Talmud and Midrash, to which H. Laible has added an introductory essay.[2] The bitterness between Jews and Christians had become very intense in Europe. Rabbi Tarphon is quoted in the Talmud [3] as saying of the Christians and the Christian writings : ' By the life of my son, should they [these Christian writings] come into my hand, I would burn them together with the names of God which they contained. Were I pursued, I would rather take refuge in a temple of idols than in their [Christians'] houses. For the latter are wilful traitors, while the heathen sinned in ignorance of the right way.' The day came when Christians burned copies of the Talmud. 'The Talmud in wagon loads was burned at Paris in 1242.' [4] Montefiore (*Judaism and St. Paul*, p. 55) says : 'When Christianity became the State Church of the Roman Empire, it was forbidden under severe penalties for anybody to become a proselyte to Judaism.' So bitter was the feeling between Jews and Christians, that in A.D. 1240, Rabbi Jechiel actually denied that the Jesus mentioned in the Talmud was Jesus of Nazareth, but modern Jews do not hold to this absurdity.[5] In order to understand the real atti-

---

[1] *Jesus in the Talmud*, p. 6.   [2] *Jesus Christus im Thalmud*, 1891.
[3] *Shabbath*, fol. 116, qt. 1.   [4] Pick, *Jesus in the Talmud*, p. 6.
[5] Levin, *Die Religionsdisputation des Rabbi Jechiel von Paris*, 1869, p. 193. Cf. also Herford, *Christianity in Talmud and Midrash*, p. 38.

tude of the Talmud toward Jesus, we must use the expurgated passages as well as the rest. The same hostility appears in the Mishna, the Tosephta (addition to the Mishna), the Gemara (commentary on the Mishna), the Midrash (homiletical literature). In fact, the height of hate is reached in the Middle Ages. 'In that period the hatred of Jesus, which was never quite dormant, begot a literature, in comparison with which the Talmud must be termed almost innocent. The *Toldoth Jeshu* literature originated, which is still continued. In the *Toldoth Jeshu* a detailed picture of the life of Jesus was put together, of which the authors of the Talmud had no anticipation.'[1] Respectable Jews are not to be held responsible for these tirades. Herford[2] is much more sympathetic with Rabbinism than is Pick or Laible, but he reproduces faithfully in English dress the work of Dalman and Laible, and does not seek to conceal the spirit of the Talmud toward Jesus.[3] There is not room to quote and discuss all the passages in the unexpurgated Talmud that refer to Jesus, but most of them are beyond dispute. The anachronisms and crass errors of fact found in the Talmudic references can only be explained on the basis of the refusal of many of the rabbis to read the Gospels or other Christian writings. Jesus is called Ben Stada and also Ben Pandira in the Talmud;[4] why we do not know, though both express contempt and mockery of Jesus.[5] Rabbi Eliezer said to the Wise : ' Did not Ben Stada bring spells from Egypt in a cut which was upon his flesh ? They said to him, He was a fool, and they do not receive proof from a fool.' Here Jesus is called a fool, and it is added that the paramour of Mary was named Pandira and the

[1] Pick, *Jesus in the Talmud*, p. 11.
[2] *Christianity in Talmud and Midrash*.
[3] *Ibid.*, p. ix. : 'My only aim is to present facts.'
[4] *Shabbath*, 104b.
[5] Herford, *Christianity in Talmud and Midrash*, pp. 38 ff. ; Pick, *Jesus in the Talmud*, pp. 14 ff. ; Origen (ap. *Epiph. Haer.*, 78).

PHARISAIC RESENTMENT TOWARD JESUS

husband was Stada. In the Mishna[1] it is stated that Jesus was a bastard, as shown by both of His pedigrees, and that Mary 'played the harlot with carpenters.'[2] Indeed, a late passage[3] claims that Mary confessed to Rabbi Akiba that Jesus was a bastard, though Rabbi Akiba lived a hundred years later.[4] Jesus is accused of practising magic, and in this we see a tacit admission of His miracles : ' Jesus the Nazarene practised magic and led astray and deceived Israel.'[5] He is accused of heresy under a figurative expression : 'That thou mayst not prove a son or disciple who burns his food in public like Jeshu the Nazarene.'[6] Herford[7] makes it plain that by this phrase the charge of heresy is conveyed. Jesus is called a liar by Rabbi Abahu :[8] ' If a man say to thee, " I am God," he is a liar ; if " the son of man," the evil people will laugh at him ; if " I will go up to heaven," he saith, but shall not perform it.' The reference to Jesus is beyond doubt, and the second and third chapters of John may be here in mind. Jesus is likened to Balaam[9] and is grouped with Balaam[10] and Titus (the three chief enemies of Israel) in hell. In some editions of the Talmud ' Jesus ' is changed here to ' the sinner of Israel.' Jesus is called ' the deceiver,' and in the case of a deceiver who tempts others to apostasy from Judaism, the concealment of witnesses to trap the accused is justified as in the case of Jesus.[11] Laible[12] holds that this species of legal procedure really rests on the trial of Jesus as reported in the Gospels. There is a curious little book by Rabbi A. P. Drucker,

[1] M. *Jeb.* iv. 13. So also b. *Joma* 66d.
[2] b. *Sanh.* 106a. [3] b. *Kallah.* 51a.
[4] Laible (*Jesus Christus im Talmud*, p. 34) denies that this passage refers to Jesus, but the Jews took it so.
[5] b. *Sanh.* 107b. [6] *Ibid.*, 103a.
[7] *Christianity in Talmud and Midrash* pp. 57 ff.
[8] j. *Taanith.* 65b. [9] M. *Sanh.* x. 2.
[10] b. *Gitt.* 56b, 57a. [11] T. *Sanh.* x. 11; b. *Sanh.* 67a.
[12] *Jesus Christus im Talmud*, p. 76.

The Trial of Jesus (1907), in which he undertakes to show by Jewish legal procedure, as given in the Talmud, that the Jewish trial of Jesus as reported in the Gospels is a myth, since in the Gospels this procedure is violated at so many points. There is a grim humour in the argument which blandly assumes that the Sanhedrin, however much they hated Jesus, could not have violated the technicalities and regularities of their own courts in order to convict Jesus. Facts are made to bend to logic and to the demands of theological controversy. But the Talmud rises up to smite Rabbi Drucker in the face. Rabbi Drucker charges Caiaphas the Sadducee with a conspiracy against Jesus and the Jewish people, and with then laying the blame on the people for killing their beloved leader! In some passages in the Talmud reference is made to the crucifixion of [1] Jesus, but once [2] it is said that Jesus was led away and stoned at Lydda, but no effort is made to blame Pontius Pilate for the death of Jesus. Certainly the Talmud adds nothing to our knowledge of Jesus, but it does show with terrible fidelity the intensity of Jewish hatred toward Christ. 'He is the deceiver, the sorcerer, the apostate, the sinner of Israel; his birth Jewish contempt blackened into disgrace, and his death is dismissed as the mere execution of a pernicious criminal.' [3]

2. *Jewish Hatred Shown in Early Christian Writings*

Justin in his *Dialogue with Trypho* gives us a vivid portrayal of how Jews felt towards Jesus in the second century A.D. ' Ye have killed the Just and His prophets before Him. And now ye despise those who hope in Him and in God, the King over all and Creator of all things, who has sent Jesus.' [4] 'The Jews hate us,

---

[1] T. *Sanh.* ix. 7.
[2] b. *Sanh.* 43a.
[3] Pick, *Jesus in the Talmud*, p. 44.
[4] *Dialogue*, 16.

because we say that Christ is already come, and because we point out that He, as had been prophesied, was crucified by them.'[1] 'In your synagogues ye curse all who have become Christians, and the same is done by the other nations, who give a practical turn to the curse, in that when any one acknowledges himself a Christian, they put him to death.'[2] 'Nay, ye have added thrusts, that Christ taught those impious, unlawful, horrible actions, which ye disseminate as charges above all against those who acknowledge Christ as Teacher and as the Son of God.'[3] 'Your teachers exhort you to permit yourselves no conversation whatever with us.'[4] 'The high priests of your nation have caused that the name of Jesus should be profaned and reviled throughout the whole world.'[5] In his *Apology*[6] Justin also says: 'The Jews regard us as foes and opponents, and kill and torture us if they have the power. In the lately ended Jewish war, Bar-Cochba, the instigator of the Jewish revolt, caused Christians alone to be dragged to terrible tortures, whenever they would not deny and revile Jesus Christ.' These quotations make very sad reading, but they at least serve to bridge the chasm between the Talmud and the New Testament, and to show the unbroken stream of Jewish resentment towards Jesus and His disciples in the early centuries.

Tertullian[7] also represents the second coming as a glorious spectacle in which he says to the Jews: 'This is your carpenter's son, your harlot's son; your Sabbath-breaker, your Samaritan, your demon-possessed! This is He whom ye bought from Judas; this is He who was struck with reeds and fists, dishonoured with spittle, and given a draught of gall and vinegar! This is He whom His disciples have stolen secretly, that it may be

[1] *Dialogue*, 35.
[2] *Ibid.*, 96.
[3] *Ibid.*, 108.
[4] *Ibid.*, 112.
[5] *Ibid.*, 117.
[6] i. 31.
[7] *De Spectaculis*, 30 (A.D. 197-8).

said He was risen, or that the gardener abstracted that his lettuces might not be damaged by the crowds of visitors!'[1] The irony is withering, almost blistering.

Origen[2] quotes from the *True Word* of Celsus charges about Jesus which Celsus had evidently learned from the Jews, and which are similar to those found in the Talmud, even to the point of saying that Jesus was Mary's son by a soldier named Panthera (or Pandira), that He learned sorcery and magic in Egypt, and gave Himself out as a god who was born of a virgin. Thus we see that the Jewish view of Jesus was widespread in the second century and was known among the heathen also.

3. *The Picture in the Acts of the Apostles*

Here the hostility towards Christians grows directly out of the claim made by Peter and John, that Jesus had indeed risen from the dead. Thus the Sadducees are stirred to the same activity against the disciples of Jesus that they had shown towards Him (Acts iv. 1-3). They were the last of the Jewish parties to be enlisted against Jesus, but the first against the disciples. The very vehemence of the Sadducaic onset against the apostles caused the Pharisees to hold aloof, and even to thwart the plans of the Sadducees for a while (Acts v. 33-42). Peter and John aroused the Sadducees, but it was Stephen who enraged the Pharisees by the same insistence on the spiritual nature of the Kingdom of God, and hence the possibility of real worship of God apart from the temple in Jerusalem, that made the Pharisees rise against Christ. Indeed, some of the same charges are made against Stephen that were made against Jesus (Acts vi. 9-14). The death of Stephen by stoning (sort

---

[1] Quoted from Pick, *Jesus in the Talmud*, pp. 10 f.
[2] i. pp. 28-32.

II.] PHARISAIC RESENTMENT TOWARD JESUS 59

of mob law) shows the unrestrained anger of the Pharisees that the heresy of Jesus, which they had hoped to destroy, is now as alive as ever, if not more so. The violent and successful persecution of the disciples by the Sanhedrin (Sadducees and Pharisees now united again as against Jesus) bears witness to deep-rooted hatred of Jesus. When Paul was converted, he was hated by the Jews with more bitterness than Peter or Stephen. Finally the mob in Jerusalem clamours for his blood as they did for that of Jesus. Before the Sanhedrin, whose agent Paul had once been, he stands unabashed and actually succeeds in setting the Pharisees and Sadducees against each other by proclaiming himself a Pharisee still on the doctrine of the resurrection of the dead, a curious example of the sudden revival of theological strife in an artificial unity. It is not pertinent to spend more time on the situation in the Acts. This sketch is given simply to show that the chain of hate is unbroken through the centuries till the Talmud is written down. The after history demands an explanation of this fierceness toward Jesus. The Gospels alone give an adequate solution of the facts of the later history, as given by both Jew and Christian. We are not here concerned with the question of who is right and who is wrong in this situation. The roots of the controversy go back to the time of Jesus, as shown in the Gospels. To be sure, Montefiore [1] tries to break the force of Paul's arraignment of Rabbinic Judaism, by saying that it ' is not Rabbinic Judaism as we know it from the Rabbinic literature and from Rabbinic life. For those criticisms, it must be remembered, are not intended to be (like the mordant criticisms of Jesus) criticisms of the perversions of Rabbinic Judaism of the defects of its qualities.' But Montefiore does not understand Paul, for Paul shows that Christianity is the true

[1] *Judaism and St. Paul*, pp. 22 f.

Judaism and Pharisaism the perversion. No doubt to Montefiore Paul 'seems often to be fighting windmills,'[1] because Montefiore takes Pharisaism to be the real Judaism, and Paul's spiritual elevation is too rarefied for him. But, this all aside, the Epistles of Paul, like the Acts, testify to the cleavage between Jew and Gentile. Paul's own heart was ready to break over it (Rom. ix. 1-3), and he clung to a future hope for the Jews (Rom. x. and xi.).

4. *The Story of Pharisaic Hate Common to all the Gospels*

The point here emphasised is, that in all Four Gospels and in the sources, as far as they can be ascertained, the Pharisees are represented as prevailingly hostile to Jesus. Perhaps Montefiore[2] may help us when he says: 'Yet we may well suppose that though Jesus believed Himself to be the predestined theocratic chief of the coming Kingdom, the political elements of the conception were still further softened down by Him or ignored. One has, however, to be careful and cautious, remembering that the Gospel records are prevailingly anti-Jewish, and, even in a certain sense, pro-Roman, and that, in view of later events and the relation of nascent Christianity to Judaism, the editing of the tradition would have been in the direction of denationalising its content and its character.' Montefiore denies the reality of the antithesis between the political Messiah of the Jews and the spiritual Messiah of Jesus, but none the less he admits that the Gospel records show a wide breach between the Pharisees and Jesus. Montefiore seeks to soften it down and blames the Gospels for adding to the antagonism. But no amount of critical pruning can explain it all away. The constant tempta-

---

[1] *Judaism and St. Paul*, p. 158.
[2] *The Religious Teaching of Jesus*, p. 131.

tion of Montefiore is to read into the mind of Jesus the theology of a moderate Jew of the present day, one who, though a Jew, feels himself an 'outsider' towards both Jews and Christians. 'I would rather think of Jesus, in the quaint words of Mr. Balmforth, as "Unitarian above all men."'[1] He says: 'I myself stand in different ways outside both sanctuaries.'[2] But this disclaimer does not remove the fact that Montefiore still looks at Jesus and the Pharisees with his 'perverse and prejudicial outsidedness,' as he facetiously terms it.[3] The story of mutual dislike between Jew and Christian, as we have traced it in Talmud, early Christian literature, the Acts of the Apostles, presupposes and necessitates an historic basis in the life of Jesus. The Gospels all testify to the reality of this animosity. Certainly it is true of the Gospel of John, whatever view one may hold of its authorship and historical value. That is still a matter of dispute among scholars, though my own view holds to the Johannine origin. The author is a Jewish Christian, who writes long after the destruction of Jerusalem, and looks back upon the tragedy of Jewish hate of Jesus in a somewhat detached and objective way, and often describes the enemies of Jesus as simply 'the Jews' (chap. vii. for instance). But, if one thinks that this Gospel reflects too much the hostile atmosphere of later Christianity towards the Jews, he will not find essential improvement in the Synoptic Gospels. In Matthew xxiii. we have the fearful woes of Jesus, as the final retort to the Pharisees for their machinations against Him. It is to be borne in mind also that the Gospel of Matthew is written with a view to showing that Jesus is the Jewish Messiah, and would naturally put as favourable a colour as possible on the relation between Jesus and the Jews. Luke was a

[1] *The Religious Teaching of Jesus*, p. 164.
[2] *Ibid.*, p. 116.   [3] *Ibid.*, p. 163.

Gentile, but he claims in his Prologue (i. 1-4) that he writes 'accurately,' and he has the historical temper. Mark is supposed to have written his Gospel in Rome, and would be charged by Montefiore with being 'pro-Roman,' but Mark's story of the death of Jesus does not differ from the rest, in the proportion of blame between Pilate and the Sanhedrin. The historical outline of Mark's Gospel is generally held to lie behind that in Luke and Matthew. If we turn to the Logia or Q, held to be the common source for the sayings of Jesus in Matthew and Luke and on a par with Mark, we find precisely the same spirit of antagonism. In Harnack's *Sayings of Jesus*, the very first paragraph given (p. 127), is the denunciation of the Jews by John the Baptist as 'offsprings of vipers' (Matt. iii. 7; Luke iii. 7). The Pharisees rejected both John and Jesus according to Q (Matt. xi. 16-19; Luke vii. 29-35). Q gives the woes of Jesus upon Chorazin and Bethsaida (Matt. xi. 21-3; Luke x. 13-15). Q gives also the accusation that Jesus cast out demons by the power of Beelzebub (Matt. xii.; Luke xi.). We need not give further proof that the earliest strata of the Gospel narratives according to modern criticism reveal the keenest antipathy of the Pharisees towards Jesus. It is the sanest historical criticism to find the solution in the facts that lie behind the unanimous testimony on the subject. It is not necessary for our purpose to contend for the accuracy of every statement on the subject in the Gospels, but simply that the facts, as already shown, justify the free use of the Four Gospels as sources for the Pharisaic resentment towards Jesus. No amount of discounting for prejudice can remove the solid basis of real antipathy that remains, and that alone explains all that follows through the centuries.

5. Some Friendly Pharisees

The essential fairness of the Gospels in the treatment of the relations between the Pharisees and Jesus may be shown by the fact that many of the Pharisees are represented as kindly disposed towards Jesus. Relatively there were good and bad Pharisees, as the Gospels show (Hughes, *Ethics of Jewish Apocryphal Literature*, p. 141). The Gospels do not make a point of blackening the Pharisees *per se*. There is discrimination shown in various ways. The Pharisees are credited, in the Gospel of John, with sending a committee of priests and Levites (Sadducees, and so with a bit of sly humour in the situation) to inquire of John the Baptist concerning his claims about himself (John i. 19-24). There is no evidence of hostility here. Jesus is allowed to teach in the synagogue at Capernaum at first without evidence of bitterness on the part of the Pharisees, though His preaching created excitement (Mark i. 21-8). Elders of the Jews, after the Pharisees as a whole have shown hostility, are pictured as coming to Jesus in behalf of the Roman centurion at Capernaum (Luke vii. 3). Jesus was invited to dine with the Pharisees in various parts of the country, though sometimes with embarrassing results. Still, the invitation was a courtesy to Jesus, and is so recorded. Probably such invitations came from the more liberal wing of the Pharisees, the school of Hillel, not from the school of Shammai.[1] Some Pharisees became disciples of Jesus or at least professed to do so, though Jesus exercised a certain caution about their approach to Him.[2] There sometimes arose a division of opinion among the Pharisees concerning Jesus, and this point is noted, as in the controversy over

---

[1] See Luke vii. 36-50; xi. 37-54; xiv. 1-24. All in Luke, please observe.
[2] Cf. Matt. viii. 19; John viii. 31.

the man born blind (John ix. 16), and at the conclusion of the allegory of the Good Shepherd, when some Pharisees boldly championed the cause of Jesus (John x. 19-21). The attitude of some of the Pharisees is noncommittal, but at least they were on decent terms with Jesus, as we see in the ambiguous advice of the Pharisees about Herod Antipas (Luke. xiii. 31 ff.), and in the query about the time when the Kingdom of God comes (Luke xvii. 20 f.). Some of the Pharisees were actually willing to blame other Pharisees for their attacks on Jesus and the futility of it all (John xii. 19): 'The Pharisees therefore said among themselves, Behold, how ye prevail nothing: lo, the world is gone after Him.' Some of the Pharisees (rulers) believed on Jesus, but lacked the courage to come out in the open on His side. 'Nevertheless even of the rulers many believed on him, but because of the Pharisees they did not confess it, lest they should be put out of the synagogue; for they loved the glory of men more than the glory of God' (John xii. 42 f.). This statement in John's Gospel throws a flood of light on the whole situation. One recalls that the parents of the man born blind refused to take the side of Jesus before the Pharisees, lest they be cast out of the synagogue, and that their son was cast out for asserting that Jesus had opened his eyes (John ix. 22, 34); Nicodemus was severely ridiculed for daring to raise a point of law in the Sanhedrin in favour of Jesus (John vii. 50-3). Joseph of Arimathea continued a secret disciple till the death of Jesus, when he boldly avowed his faith in the dead Christ (John xix. 38-40). Nicodemus also now openly took his stand for Jesus, these two Pharisees and members of the Sanhedrin. It must not then be overlooked that, difficult as it finally became for Pharisees to espouse the side of Jesus, some did it, while many others secretly loved Him and wished Him well. It is to be recalled also that later Gamaliel, grandson and successor of Hillel, showed a kindly spirit towards Peter and John, before Stephen aroused the animosity of the Pharisees. If there is prejudice in the Gospels against the Pharisees, it is not blind prejudice that can see no good in them at all.

6. *Presumption against Jesus because of John the Baptist*

We now come to the heart of the subject, but all the preceding discussion has been necessary to enable us to understand the elements in the situation. The Pharisees meet Jesus and the issue is joined between them almost instinctively. From the very start the majority of the leaders are suspicious and finally become violent and desperate. We must now take up the various counts which the Pharisees find against Jesus. It is an astonishing array, as the records in the Gospels give them, but the survey will repay our attention. Of course we must understand here, as in all controversy, that all is not said. Often the deepest motives that prompt to action are unexpressed, but usually what is said makes clear what the real animus is. The total result will make all clear enough. John the Baptist had already incurred the hatred of the Pharisees, who were thus to a certain extent prejudiced against Jesus. Luke (iii. 7) merely speaks of the 'multitude' that went out to be baptized of John, more precisely 'the multitudes' (τοῖς ὄχλοις) or 'the crowds' as Moffatt puts it. But Matthew specifically singles out 'many of the Pharisees and Sadducees' as the occasion for the sharp words of John. Plummer[1] suggests that both Matthew and Luke here quote from *Memoirs of the Baptist* (part of Harnack's Q), and that Matthew has preserved the original form better, which is more suit-

[1] *Commentary on Matthew*, p. 27.

able to the Pharisees and Sadducees. The epithet 'offspring of vipers' or 'brood of snakes' (γεννήματα ἐχιδνῶν) fleeing from the wrath to come, may have been suggested to John by 'snakes flying before a prairie-fire'[1] which John had seen in the wilderness. At any rate the words stuck like burrs, and were never forgotten by the Pharisees, who would hold them against John the Baptist. The use of these very words later by Jesus would be like a blow on an old wound (Matt. xii. 34; xxiii. 33). John's references to the Messiah were at first in general terms, and his later identification of Jesus as the Messiah may not have impressed the Pharisees (John i. 26, 29-37). When the Pharisees first saw Jesus they did not apparently associate Him with John, but it was not long before they did so (John iv 1-4).

7. *Grounds of Pharisaic Dislike of Jesus*

Numerous specific complaints are filed against Jesus by the Pharisees. Let us see what they are.

(1) *Assumption of Messianic Authority* (John ii. 13-22)

The assertion of authority by Jesus in the temple at once enraged the ecclesiastics. This incident is recorded only by John, and is similar to the cleansing of the temple at the close of the public ministry, as reported by the Synoptic Gospels. Many scholars regard it as the same event, which is out of place in John, but it seems to me more natural to follow John's chronology and to admit a repetition at the close. Only thus can we properly see the growth of hostility toward Jesus in Jerusalem so vividly narrated in John's Gospel. It was inevitable that the soul of Jesus should cry out against this desecration of His Father's house when He first appeared in the temple after entering upon His Messianic ministry. It may be straining the point to insist that

[1] *Commentary on Matthew*, p. 27.

the Pharisees are involved in the protest on the part of
the Jews. The house of Hanan (Annas) carried on a
regular market in the outer court of the temple (τὸ ἱερόν),
and Annas was a Sadducee. The priests who had charge
of the temple ritual were chiefly Sadducees, while the
Pharisees found their chief forte and function in the
synagogue. But the Pharisees were strong in the
Sanhedrin, and the sacerdotal abuses in the temple
worship, where graft of all kinds was notorious, could
have been exposed by the Pharisees and stopped by
public opinion. Jesus did arraign the leaders, and for
the moment cleansed the temple by a supreme act of
personal power and Messianic worth. But He received
no support from the Pharisees in this onslaught on the
corruption of the Sadducees. By 'the Jews' (John ii.
18, 20) John's Gospel usually means the hostile Jews,
whether Pharisees or Sadducees. At any rate, the
ecclesiastics in Jerusalem, probably both Pharisees and
Sadducees, resent the interference in the established
order of things by an uncouth interloper from Galilee.
The demand for a sign implied more than a mere miracle.
It reached to the core of the Messianic claim of Jesus,
and at once placed Him on the defensive. The defence
of Jesus when the demand for His ecclesiastical authority
or Divine sanction was made, as there was a technical
right for making it, only enraged them all the more,
and in a mutilated form it was cherished against Him
till His trial, that He had threatened to destroy the
temple with the foolish claim that He could rebuild it
in three days. This first clash with the Jerusalem
authorities revealed to Jesus the hopeless breach between
Him and the religious leaders of His day. At once it
was apparent that the custodians of the Torah, whether
priest or scribe, would oppose real reform, and any
effort to set up spiritual life in the empty shell of current
Judaism. The very timidity of Nicodemus, a leading

Pharisee and member of the Sanhedrin (John iii.), shows that the Pharisees as a class at once took ground in opposition to the claims of Jesus, in spite of the courteous 'we know' of Nicodemus (John iii. 2), probably a mere literary plural. It was intolerable to the Pharisees that a man should by deed or word make Messianic claims without consultation with the scribes, the authorised teachers of the written and oral law. The rabbis had some divergences in their views about the Messiah, but they all agreed on the point of their own importance as interpreters of the subject. At the very first then Jesus was an ignorant upstart to the Pharisees, who was in revolutionary fashion upsetting all precedents and disturbing the religious order and peace of the people, not to mention His infringement of the vested rights of the merchants and bankers in the temple courts.

The Sanhedrin, Pharisees (scribes) and Sadducees (chief priests), also challenged the authority of Jesus in a formal manner on the last day of Christ's public ministry, the Tuesday of Passion Week. As a matter of fact, Jesus had no ecclesiastical standing from their standpoint, but was a mere layman, as we should say. He had the baptism of John who was sent of God, but Divine sanction was not sufficient before the great Jewish ecclesiastical court. Something more than the approval of God was required. But Jesus in a marvellous way parried their attack by demanding their opinion of the baptism of John. This question was quite to the point, and broke the effect of their demand. They were helpless in the dilemma between fear of Jesus and the fear of the multitude.

But let us return to the situation in Jerusalem and Judea after the collision with the authorities at the first passover, as recorded in John's Gospel. Westcott [1] notes that John's Gospel never mentions the Sadducees

[1] Commentary *in loco*.

or Herodians by name, since the Pharisees are the real representatives of the Jewish nation. So here the Pharisees were jealously watching the rapid growth of the popularity of Jesus, the new Prophet who had followed so close upon the heels of John the Baptist. The tremendous sweep and power of the Baptist's work were all too fresh in their minds. They could still feel the sting of His words as He whipped them in the face before the crowds, and made their cheeks burn with shame as he laid bare their hypocrisy and ceremonial absurdities. But the Pharisees now found satisfaction in the arrest of John by Herod Antipas and his incarceration in Machaerus. It is not clear what the Pharisees did to get John involved with Herod. It is possible that they may have had him invited into the presence of Herod, and then asked John's opinion about divorce, as they tempted Jesus on this subject much later (Matt. xix. 3 ; Mark x. 2), knowing full well that he was too brave to flinch even in the presence of the Tetrarch. At all events, none rejoiced more heartily over the fate of the Baptist than did the Pharisees. They watched the rising tide of the power of Jesus. As John went, so must Jesus go. It is probable that the attitude of the Pharisees was by this time well known to close observers. Jesus promptly saw that the combination of John's imprisonment and his own great popularity with the people made Judea a dangerous place for Him to pursue His work, unless He was ready for the final issue. This Jesus did not wish, for His hour of supreme crisis had not yet come. From now on there is no doubt about Pharisaic opposition to Jesus, though as yet no formal charges are filed against Him, save the general one of the usurpation of the Messianic prerogative without ecclesiastical permission or Divine sanction (John ii. 19). The truth is, that already the Pharisees have weighed Jesus and found Him wanting.

They had rejoiced for a season in the light of John the
Baptist (John v. 35), and even went so far as to send a
formal committee from the Sanhedrin, to investigate
his claims about himself (John i. 19-26), but the
Pharisees seem never to have shown that much consideration for Jesus. John had in truth more points
of contact with the Pharisees [1] than had Jesus, as is
shown also by the fact that some of the disciples of
John joined with the Pharisees in criticism of Jesus
(Mark viii. 18), and by the fear that the Pharisees had
for John's power over the people to the end (Matt. xxi.
26). And yet the Pharisees in reality hated John with
bitterness, and rejected His baptism (Luke vii. 30) as
an indictment of all Israel, as if they were heathen and
had derived no benefit from being descendents of
Abraham. The precise counts against Jesus will develop
in due order. Herford [2] frankly admits that the Pharisees
properly seized the issue between them and Jesus.
'That the Pharisees knew why they feared, distrusted,
and finally helped to destroy Jesus is true enough. And
Jesus expressed, in the plainest terms, the ground on
which He denounced the Pharisees. But whether on
either side the real significance of the struggle was
clearly seen, is to my mind doubtful. Jesus may have
seen it. I do not think the Pharisees did, or ever have
done, from that day to this.' It is certain that Jesus
saw at once the issue and how to meet it. The Pharisees
also at once saw that they must suppress Jesus or perish,
though it was probably vague to them why it was so.
As Herford says, the Pharisees are still in the dark on
that subject. 'To the Pharisees He appeared as a
sort of unregistered practitioner.' [3] It was 'inevitable
that they should regard Him as a dangerous heretic.' [4]
'Jesus was condemned and executed on a more or less

---

[1] Westcott, John iv. 1.   [2] *Pharisaism*, pp. 127 f.
[3] *Ibid.*, p. 131.   [4] *Ibid.*, p. 143.

PHARISAIC RESENTMENT TOWARD JESUS

political charge, for which the question of Messiahship provided a useful basis; but was really rejected, so far at all events as the Pharisees were concerned, because He undermined the authority of the Torah, and endangered the religion founded upon it.'[1] Thus Herford[2] sums up the Pharisaic instinct toward Jesus: 'Torah and Jesus could not remain in harmony. The two were fundamentally incompatible.' The Pharisees felt as if a burglar had invaded their house and was about to set it on fire. So Jesus withdrew from Judea to Galilee. Will the Pharisees leave Him alone in Galilee?

(2) *Downright Blasphemy* (Luke v. 17-26; John v. 18; x. 22-42; Matt. xxvi. 65; Mark xiv. 64)

Soon Pharisaic inspectors appear in Galilee also. The independence of Jesus quickly set tongues to wagging in Capernaum. 'What is this? a new teaching!' (Mark i. 27). The rabbis had never talked in that fashion free from rabbinical rules and fresh with the dew of heaven. The Pharisees had followed the people when all Judea and Jerusalem went out to hear John the Baptist. So now the 'Pharisees and doctors of the law' came to Capernaum out of every village of Galilee and Judea and Jerusalem' (please note Jerusalem) and 'were sitting by' to see for themselves what would happen. They had not long to wait, for 'the power of the Lord was with him to heal.' In this instance Jesus forgave the man's sins before He healed the poor paralytic. The scribes and the Pharisees began to reason in their hearts, and at once found fault with the assumption of a Divine prerogative on the part of Jesus, the power and authority ($\dot{\epsilon}\xi o \upsilon \sigma \acute{\iota} a$) to forgive sins. Their mood is hostile and Jesus feels it, and finally within themselves some say: 'This man blasphemeth' (Matt. ix. 3). Here is a clash of spirit with spirit. This is the

[1] *Pharisaism*, p. 143. [2] *Ibid.*, p. 146.

real conflict between Jesus and the Pharisees. Jesus is the incarnation of the spirit of love, pity, sympathy, help. The Pharisees stand for the regulated order of things as they are, the form and constituted authority even at the expense of life and love. The Pharisees strike at Jesus by blind instinct, and accuse Him of blasphemy, because He exercises the functions of God in forgiving sin and restoring spiritual life and health to the man. The Pharisees did not agree among themselves as to how the atonement for sin was made and remission secured, but the method usually included sacrifice and ritual purification whether repentance was present or not (Oesterley, *Religion and Worship of the Synagogue*, pp. 263-7, 279). At any rate, forgiveness was not a matter to be so lightly handled as Jesus seemed to do. 'Rabbinism stood confessedly silent and groundless, as regarded the forgiveness of sins' (Edersheim, *Life and Times of Jesus the Messiah*, vol. i. p. 508). Jesus defies the Pharisees, and accepts their challenge, and makes a virtual claim to deity : [1] 'But that ye may know that the Son of man hath power on earth to forgive sins, I say unto thee, Arise, take up thy bed, and go into thy house.' The intolerable part of it all was that the man 'straightway took up the bed, and went forth before them all' (Mark ii. 12). Now the Pharisees had a definite charge to make against Jesus, and one of which they were themselves witnesses. He was a blasphemer. To be sure, He had embarrassed them greatly by healing the paralytic as proof of His right to forgive sins. But the miracle was another question. That problem must be attacked, but one thing at a time. The enthusiasm of the public on this occasion made it necessary for the Pharisees to observe

---

[1] And this is in the Synoptic Gospels (Matt. ix. 6 ; Mark ii. 10 ; Luke v. 24). The interjected parenthesis 'he saith to the sick of the palsy' appears in each of the Synoptics and argues for a common source here.

the decencies for the present. They could bide their time and would not forget this incident and this item of proof against the new enemy of the Pharisaic order. Against the interpretation of M'Neile (Matt. ix. 6) that Jesus merely speaks of Himself as man, and that any man has the right to forgive sins, is to be placed the fact that the Pharisees did not claim the right to forgive sins, but called it a divine function. Jesus accepts their presentation and applies it to Himself as the Son of Man, not as any man. But the point to keep in mind is that the Pharisees are now in Galilee in great numbers. Apparently those from Jerusalem have come in a more or less representative capacity as a result of reports that came to headquarters in Jerusalem concerning the tremendous effect of the work of Jesus in Galilee. The Pharisees see clearly that the withdrawal of Jesus to Galilee has simply changed the scene of His activity and is not the end.

This charge of blasphemy sprang out of the claim of Jesus to work on the Sabbath, as God does, and from the claim that God is His Father in a sense not true of other men. He made this claim in justification of His healing the impotent man on the Sabbath day in Jerusalem. The Pharisees 'sought the more to kill him, because he not only brake the Sabbath, but also called God his own Father, making himself equal with God' (John v. 18). Jesus thus maintained that He was the Son of God, and proceeded to defend this supreme claim in a powerful apologetic (John v. 19-47). But this charge of blasphemy was repeated. At the feast of dedication about three months before His death, the Jews in the temple flung it at Him in these words : 'For a good work we stone thee not, but for blasphemy ; and because that thou, being a man, makest thyself God' (John x. 33). The Roman emperors were posing as gods and receiving worship. The Pharisees mean to say that Jesus also is assuming the prerogatives of God, and is thus guilty of blasphemy. The reply of Jesus is not a disclaimer of His deity, but a retort in kind (*argumentum ad hominem*), to show that in the Old Testament itself (Psalm lxxxii. 6) the term 'god' was applied to those who exercised the functions of God at His command. Thus He cut the ground from under them for the time being. But Jesus knew clearly that His enemies would repeat the charge, and so left Jerusalem for Perea.

The Messianic demonstration (triumphal entry) enraged the Pharisees intensely. They saw in this popular approval the frustration of all their plans for His death. Some in despair went to abusing each other for their common failure (John xii. 19). Others sought to make Jesus ashamed of the conduct of the multitude of Christ's disciples, in publicly hailing Him as the Son of David (Messiah), with the implication that He would disavow their enthusiasm (Luke xix. 39). But Jesus' hour had now come for His public claim to Messiahship. If need be, the very stones would now cry out in His behalf. Still others (chief priests and scribes) in the temple itself were indignant that Jesus allowed the boys (παῖδες) to desecrate the sacred precincts of the temple (their temple) by crying 'Hosannah to the Son of David.' Even the boys had been led astray by the bad example of the Galilean mob, and were misbehaving in the temple itself (Matt. xxi. 15 f.) M'Neile (Matt. *in loco*) considers it 'extremely improbable' that boys would be allowed to shout in the temple. But boys do things before they are allowed. Plummer (Matt. *in loco*) rightly notes the horror of the hierarchy at this profanation by the boys, echoing the shouts of the multitude, in contrast with the complacent acquiescence in the profitable traffic in the same courts.

The penalty for blasphemy was death by stoning. The victim was then to be hung on a gibbet and taken down before night (Lev. xxiv. 16 ; 1 Kings xxi. 10, 13). It was on the charge of blasphemy that the vote of condemnation was taken in the Sanhedrin. Jesus, after the Sanhedrin had failed to prove any charge against him, confessed on oath, in reply to a direct question from Caiaphas, that He was the Messiah the Son of God (Matt. xxvi. 63 f. ; Mark xiv. 61 f.). It was not blasphemy to be the Messiah, if it was true. Not all the Pharisees ascribed divine prerogatives to the Messiah. But Jesus evidently claimed that position for Himself by the term 'the Son of God.' The high priest was expected (Plummer on Matt. *in loco*) to rend His clothes when a gross offence against God took place in His presence (Lev. xxi. 10). It is remarkable that at the trial of Jesus the Sanhedrin make such a pitiful showing after making so many charges against Him during His ministry. The only one that will stand before their own court is this one of blasphemy, which is supplied by Jesus Himself, and is only valid on the assumption that He is not the Messiah, the Son of God. The high priest exulted in the fact that there was fortunately no further need of witnesses : ' For we ourselves have heard from his own mouth ' (Luke xxii. 71). Jesus had said that the Sanhedrin would see Him sitting at the right hand of power (Matt. xxvi. 64). It was not blasphemy in the sense of saying something against God (M'Neile), but only in the Divine claims made for Himself. When finally Pilate surrendered to the Sanhedrin after his repeated protestations of the innocence of Jesus so far as Roman law was concerned, and made his petulant exposure of his own incapacity, saying : ' Take him yourselves, and crucify him, for I find no crime in him ' (John xix. 6), the Sanhedrin quickly retorted : ' We have a law, and for that law he ought to die, because he made himself the Son of God.' They had not told Pilate of their previous condemnation on the charge

of blasphemy, and this statement of Jesus' claim made
him more afraid than ever. Whatever support Jesus
may have had in the Sanhedrin up to this point vanished
when He made His great confession (M'Neile on Matt.)
There was no proposal to test the claim of Jesus to be
divine (Swete on Mark). That was assumed as false.
It is probable that Joseph of Arimathea and Nicodemus
were not summoned to the meeting. As Jesus hung
on the cross the Pharisees mocked Him for saying ' I
am the Son of God ' (Matt. xxvii. 43).

(3) *Intolerable Association with Publicans and Sinners*
(Matt. ix. 10 ff. ; Mark ii. 15 ff. ; Luke v. 29 ff. ;
vii. 29 ; xv. 1-32)

In order to understand the feeling of the Pharisees
toward Jesus for His free mingling with publicans and
sinners, one has only to recall their assumption of
extraordinary sanctity and professions of ceremonial
purity, as set forth in the preceding chapter. As shown
by their own writings (the Psalms of Solomon, the
Talmud, etc.), the Pharisees had a perfect horror of contamination from association with the masses of the
people, the untutored '*Am-ha-'arets*, and regarded the
rest of the people as sinners in comparison with themselves (the righteous). Jesus not merely associated
with the masses in utter violation of the Pharisaic
teaching as to separation and ceremonial cleanness, but
He went among the diseased and the immoral in His
efforts to heal body and soul. Their scorn was expressed
in the phrase ' publicans and sinners,' as the familiar
companions of Jesus, with the implication that He was
no better than His associates. This high plea for
Pharisaic puritanism did not always imply moral cleanness, but did demand religious purity, a very different

matter. The Pharisees really reflected the attitude of the Jewish people in their insistence on fidelity to the Torah. Their aim was to make 'the whole people a people of the law'[1] and the law as interpreted by the Pharisees. Schuerer adds: 'The common man was to know what the law commanded, and not only to know, but to do it.' Hence the Pharisaic contempt for 'this multitude which knoweth not the law' (John vii. 49). Hence their rage at Jesus for His defiance of their scruples and practices, which involved their whole creed and conduct. The Talmud does speak a deal about repentance, but as 'only another form of work-righteousness,'[2] and 'Rabbinism had no welcome to the sinner' till he had cleansed himself ceremonially before God and man. Indeed, 'the last word of Rabbinism is only a kind of Pessimism' (Edersheim, *Life and Times*, vol. i. p. 513), and the best he could expect was to die before he sinned again (*Ab. Zar.* 17a). When therefore the Pharisees saw Jesus surrounded by 'publicans and sinners' at the feast given in His honour by Levi (Matt.), the converted publican, they were very indignant. M'Neile[3] thinks that Jesus was the host, rather than Levi, and Himself invited the publicans and sinners, since Levi would hardly have invited such a motley crew to meet Jesus. But Levi probably knew the reputation of Jesus on this very point already, and certainly He had asked Levi to follow Him. The term 'sinner' ($\dot{a}\mu\alpha\rho\tau\omega\lambda\dot{o}s$) had a wide application as an expression of Jewish scorn, not only to the openly immoral (Luke vii. 37), but to Gentiles as a class (Gal. ii. 15), to heretics (John ix. 16, 31), to publicans (custom-house officers) as a class (Luke xix. 7), and even to Jesus himself (John ix. 24). In the Psalms of the

---

[1] Schuerer, div. ii. vol. ii. p. 90.
[2] Edersheim, *Life and Times*, vol. i. p. 509.
[3] Matt. *in loco*.

Pharisees, the term includes Sadducees as well as all non-Pharisees. Hellenising Jews are so called in 1 Macc. ii. 44, 48. According to eastern custom it was possible for the Pharisees to enter the house during a reception (meal) without an invitation.[1] The banqueting hall stood open, and they could easily slip in if they cared not for the ceremonial pollution. Curiosity to get proof against Jesus may have overcome their scruples in that case. Even Pharisaic Christians were opposed to eating with Gentiles (Acts xi. 3), and these Pharisees may have been unwilling to enter the house of a publican like Levi. In that case they either stood on the outside and made remarks to the disciples as they came out or spoke to them later about it. The Pharisees had learnt some caution [2] by this time, and addressed their criticism to the disciples, not to Jesus. But Jesus took it up and answered it, for He was the real point of attack, and the disciples had simply followed His lead in the matter. They had accused Jesus of departing from the moral standard of the Old Testament (Psalm i.). It was a keen criticism and one not easy to answer. Every minister of the Gospel to-day has to face precisely this peril, if he goes among the outcast classes and does not exercise proper prudence in the way in which he carries on his task. The reply of Jesus was quite unexpected and disconcerting, but absolutely crushing. He, for the sake of argument, took the Pharisees at the face value of their claim to be 'righteous,' and asserted His mission, as the physician of souls, to the sinful, and therefore precisely to the publicans and sinners. The Pharisees had criticised Him therefore for doing His real work. At once it is clear that Jesus and the Pharisees stand at opposite

---

[1] Trench, *Parables*, p. 302 n.; Tristram, *Eastern Customs in Bible Lands*, p. 36.
[2] Swete, Mark ii. 16.

poles of thought in their attitude towards men and the work of rescue. They were aloof in spirit, and built a hedge around themselves to keep off infection. Jesus plunged into the midst of disease and sin to root both out. He admits the danger and glories in it. Not yet have all Christians come to feel as Jesus did on this subject. Jesus appealed to Hosea vi. 6 (' I desire mercy, and not sacrifice ') in proof of the failure of the Pharisees to understand the very Scriptures which they had accused Him of violating. But Jesus came to glory in the taunt flung at Him by the Pharisees (Luke vii. 34) as 'the friend of publicans and sinners,' though they probably gave a sinister meaning to 'friend' ($\phi\iota\lambda$os), as boon-companion and sharer in their vices.

It was inevitable that this charge should be repeated, since Jesus would not change His conduct in so fundamental a matter, and the Pharisees would not alter their attitude, could not, in fact, without a violent intellectual revolution. The next time this accusation is made against Jesus by a Pharisee, it is in a Pharisee's house, probably in Galilee. Jesus was there at the invitation of this Pharisee, but the host could not brook the conduct of his guest, whom he probably thought he had highly honoured by his courtesy. He may indeed have prided himself on this show of independence (Plummer on Luke vii. 36) of the Pharisaic leaders, who were now so hostile to Jesus. The sinful woman had followed oriental custom in entering the Pharisee's house uninvited. The Pharisee showed no surprise or displeasure at her presence, but only astonishment that Jesus allowed her to wet His feet with her tears, and to wipe them with her hair. The Pharisee Simon knew her general reputation as a sinner, but did not know of her penitence. Here again the Pharisee, with his insistence on outward form, in his heart assails Jesus, who cares more for the inward change of heart as seen in the woman's great love. Jesus dared to violate the conventional proprieties, and to incur the secret ridicule of His host.

Jesus had taken His stand as the friend of the publicans and sinners, and gradually overcame the timidity of those classes that had been shrinking from the rabbis, who held themselves aloof as from a pestilence. Luke (xv. 1) pointedly says: 'Now all the publicans and sinners were drawing near unto him for to hear him.' It was now a custom ($ἦσαν\ ἐγγίζοντες$) on the part of all of both classes when Jesus was around. They were no longer afraid of Him as they were of the other rabbis. Here is a lesson for the modern preacher, to learn how to win the sinful to Jesus without any sacrifice of purity of life and not to drive them away by affectation of much righteousness. Real goodness does rebuke sin, but it is attractive to the sinner. Luke does not locate the incident that called forth the wonderful parables in chap. xv. of his Gospel. It was probably in Perea, but, wherever it was, the Pharisees resented the conduct of Jesus in allowing these despised classes to crowd close around Him, with the result that the Pharisees, in self-defence and for decency's sake, stood off at a distance and gave the publicans and sinners the right of way. The Pharisees had no gospel to the lost. 'They had nothing to say to sinners. They called upon them to "do penitence" and then Divine Mercy, or rather Justice, would have its reward for the penitent.'[1] There is no indication that on this occasion Jesus was eating with publicans and sinners, but He had done so at Levi's reception (Matt. ix. 10 f.). They make a double charge here: 'This man receiveth sinners and eateth with them' ($οὗτος\ ἁμαρτωλοὺς\ προσδέχεται\ καὶ\ συνεσθίει\ αὐτοῖς$). Jesus not only allowed them access, but He actually welcomed them. He not only saluted them and talked with them in public as respectable people, but He

---

[1] Edersheim, *Life and Times*, vol. ii. p. 253.

even ate with them on terms of social equality. The thing was intolerable in the eyes of the Pharisees, who 'murmured' a great deal, and kept up a buzz of discontent (διεγόγγυζον). The scribes joined with the Pharisees in this protest. It was against both precept and practice and could not be overlooked. They made thus a formal and public challenge of the position of Jesus and His conduct, no longer to the disciples or in the secret thoughts. Jesus did not deny the charge. He admitted it, justified it, and even extended it. He was engaged in the precise business of seeking and saving the lost. If the publicans and sinners did not come to Jesus, He would go after them. The cry of the one lost lamb in the hills would give the shepherd no peace, even though the ninety and nine were safe within the fold. Here again the reply of Jesus completely turns the tables on His enemies, who only grew angrier than ever. Finally 'they scoffed at him' (ἐξεμυκτήριζον αὐτόν, turned the nose up at Him) after Jesus told the parable of the unjust steward.

(4) *Irreligious Neglect of Fasting* (Matt. ix. 14-17; Mark ii. 18-22; Luke v. 33-9)

The charge about the neglect of fasting follows the feast of Levi, and the charge about eating with publicans and sinners. The regular public fasts of the Jews in the Old Testament are only five,[1] but the Pharisees made a good deal out of private fasting, like the Pharisee in Luke xviii. 12, who boasted of his piety in this respect. But this private Pharisaic fasting was done in public to be seen of men (Matt. vi. 16), and they even disfigured their faces to show that they were fasting. It was said of John the Baptist that he 'came neither eating nor drinking,' and yet the Pharisees rejected

[1] Oesterley, *Religion and Worship of the Synagogue*, p. 433.

John's baptism, and scoffed at his asceticism (Luke vii. 30, 33) as though he had a demon, while they reviled Jesus as 'a gluttonous man, and a wine-bibber, a friend of publicans and sinners' (vii. 34). But the ascetic habits of John led his disciples to find an affinity with the Pharisees in the matter of fasting, especially while John was himself in prison. They perhaps were all the more ready to criticise Jesus if Levi's feast came at the time of one of the fast days. In Mark ii. 18 John's disciples and the Pharisees are said to be fasting, and both together came to Jesus, with the query why His disciples do not fast. In Matthew and Luke the disciples of John are the speakers. Perhaps they acted as catspaws for the Pharisees, but it is sad to see this combination of the disciples of John with the enemies of Jesus. The question raised is treated in a serious manner by Jesus, who uses it to illustrate the fundamental difference between the new life of the Kingdom and the old order of rite and ceremony which was to pass away. There is a connection between Christianity and Judaism, but it is the Judaism of the heart, Paul's circumcision of the heart, not of the flesh, the spiritual Israel. This new wine needs new wineskins. This new piece cannot be patched on an old garment. The bridegroom is still with the bride. It will be time enough to fast when He is taken away, as John, alas! has been. Fasting with Jesus is an individual act for a real reason, not a stated function for empty show. But here again professional Pharisaism cannot brook the independence of this revolutionary thinker who is cutting the ground from under their feet, and making their whole system appear ridiculous in the eyes of the people.

II.] PHARISAIC RESENTMENT TOWARD JESUS 83

(5) *The Devil Incarnate or in league with Beelzebub*
(Matt. ix. 34 ; xii. 22-37 ; Mark iii. 19-30 ; Luke
xi. 14-36)

This bitter charge that Jesus was in league with the
devil came early in the Galilean ministry, as a result
of the enthusiasm of the multitude who 'marvelled,
saying, It was never so seen in Israel' (Matt. ix. 34).
This itself was a reflection on the Pharisees, and placed
the crown on the head of Jesus as the supreme teacher
who acted as well as spoke. M'Neile (on Matt. ix. 34)
treats this verse as 'a scribal insertion due to xii. 24 ;
Luke xi. 15,' and Plummer (on Matt. ix. 34) rather
inclines to the view that we have here a doublet.[1] If so,
we only know that the Pharisees are not recorded as
giving expression to their venom on the subject quite
so early. 'By the prince of the demons casteth he
out demons.' There is no effort to deny the reality of
the casting out. The Pharisees are content to find the
source of this kind of miracle in the devil himself. In
Matt. xii. 22-37 the multitudes not only 'were amazed'
(ἐξίσταντο, stood out of themselves with astonishment,
like the eyes standing out of the head), but they actually
dared to ask: 'Is this the Son of David?' They
asked it in a form (μήτι οὗτός ἐστιν ὁ υἱὸς Δαυείδ;)
that implied a negative answer, but this may have been
due to a desire to avoid controversy rather than to the
conviction that it was not true. The Pharisees evidently
felt that the very fact of such an inquiry from the
astonished crowds showed that the claims and miracles
of Jesus had produced such an effect on the people
that they were ready to hail Him as the Messiah, the
Son of David. This of all things was what the Pharisees
did not wish to happen. They saw clearly by this time

[1] It is wanting in D a d Syr Sin.

that the conception of the Kingdom held by Jesus was subversive of Pharisaic theology. Jesus taught that the King-Messiah was non-political, and offered no hope to the Jews of freedom from the Roman yoke, but only a vague spiritual rule of God in the heart, for which the rabbis did not care, without the political hope of place and power. The charge as stated here is: 'This man doth not cast out demons, but by Beelzebub, the prince of the demons.' There is probably a slur in the use of 'this man' (οὗτος), and the negative form of the statement discounts it as far as they can. He is only able to do what He does because He has the help of Beelzebub. The demons in reality receive orders from their chief, whose agent Jesus is. This whole subject of demonology is difficult, but there was no doubt on the part of the Pharisees as to the existence of the devil and his demons. The recent war in Europe makes it easier for modern men to see how the devil and demons may still have power over men. But the charge springs out of spite against Jesus, and is meant to ruin His power with the people by prejudicing their minds against Him in spite of His power to work miracles. The reply of Jesus exposes their blindness, for the devil would not destroy his own work. Satan does not cast out Satan, and is not divided against himself. This retort left the Pharisees without an answer, and the multitude evidently saw the force of the reply of Christ. By and by some of the Pharisees themselves will be so impressed that they will ask: 'Can a demon open the eyes of the blind?' (John x. 21). And yet many of the Pharisees at Jerusalem had become so angered with Jesus, that they had in a rage said the two meanest things that they could think of for the moment: 'Say we not well that thou art a Samaritan, and hast a demon (John viii. 48)?' That combination to the Pharisee was the acme of shame in this world and the next. Neither epithet was true as applied to Jesus, but the use of them both relieved the feelings of the Pharisees. Many of them repeat the accusation after the allegory of the Good Shepherd, in which the Pharisees are described as thieves and robbers, and say : ' He hath a demon and is mad ' (John viii. 20). It was charitable to treat Jesus as insane. Some modern German critics have called Jesus a paranoiac.[1] The same charge of demoniacal agency is given by Luke (xi. 14-38), and belongs to a later Perean ministry if Luke's narrative is not merely a duplicate of that in Matthew and Mark. It is not improbable that the Pharisees should repeat this charge. Indeed, we have seen that the Talmud makes precisely the same explanation of the signs wrought by Jesus. It shows how malignant the Pharisaic leaders have become in their resentment and anger.

(6) *A Regular Sabbath Breaker* (John v. ; Matt. xii. 1-14 ; Mark ii. 23, iii. 6 ; Luke vi. 1-11 ; John ix. ; Luke xiii. 10-21 ; xiv. 1-24)

We have only to recall the Pharisaic rules for the observance of the Sabbath to see how sensitive the Pharisees were on this subject. Thomson (*Int. Stand. Bible Encycl.*) thinks that the Pharisees at first hoped to win Jesus over to their side. They would have been only too willing to accept Him as Messiah with all His miracles and popular favour, provided He would conform to the Pharisaic pattern for the Messiah. This involved the acceptance of the teachings of the scribes and the practice of the Pharisees. Thomson interprets the invitations from the Pharisees to dine as an effort to cajole Jesus into compliance with the plans of the Pharisees, ' which was going far upon the part of a

[1] Schaefer, *Jesus in psychiatrischer Beleuchtung* (1910); Werner, *Die Psychische Gesundheit* (1908).

Pharisee toward one not a *ḥābhēr*. Even when He hung on the cross, the taunt with which they greeted Him may have had something of longing, lingering hope in it : " If He be the King of Israel, let Him now come down from the cross, and we will believe on Him " (Matt. xxvii. 42).' Some of the Pharisees who demanded signs may have secretly hoped that He would do the spectacular signs which the rabbis had outlined as proof of the Messiah, so that the Pharisees could with better grace hail Him as the Messiah of Pharisaism. But this critical attitude that lingered with some Pharisees was not shared by the leaders, who quickly, as we have seen, became distinctly adverse. The conduct of Jesus on the Sabbath day and His justification of His conduct exasperated the Pharisees exceedingly. The matters of detail were so obvious and so public that there was no escape from a clash if the Pharisees held their ground on this subject. They had to criticise Jesus or stultify themselves in the eyes of the masses. The first instance of healing on the Sabbath created astonishment, but called forth no protest from the Pharisees so far as the records show (Mark i. 21-8 ; Luke iv. 31-7). But this was in Galilee, and the Pharisaic campaign against Jesus had not yet begun in that region. But when Jesus healed the man at the Pool of Bethesda in Jerusalem on the Sabbath, a storm of protest arose when the poor fellow told the Jews that Jesus had made him whole, and had bidden him to carry his bed (pallet, κράβαττον, bed of the poor) on the Sabbath. ' For this cause did the Jews persecute Jesus, because He did these things on the Sabbath ' (John v. 16). This was the first occasion when the Jews began to persecute (ἐδίωκον, inchoative imperfect) Jesus, but He already had the habit of doing (ἐποίει) these and like things on the Sabbath. Hence the violence of the explosion of Pharisaic wrath on this occasion. Besides, it was in

II.] PHARISAIC RESENTMENT TOWARD JESUS 87

Jerusalem, near the temple and possibly at a passover. The enmity of the Pharisees was already 'settled' (Westcott *in loco*). The defence of Jesus made it worse, for it was a virtual claim of equality with God and the Son of God in a sense not true of others. He deserved, they held, to be stoned as a common Sabbath-breaker, and all the more so since He made such blasphemous claims about His peculiar right to violate the Pharisaic Sabbatic laws (John v. 17 f.). It is a bit curious to note that the rabbis had been puzzled over the fact that Jesus here cites the continuous activity of God on the Sabbath in spite of the Pharisaic rules on the subject. 'Why does not God keep the Sabbath? May not a man wander through his own house on the Sabbath? The house of God is the whole realm above and the whole realm below.'[1] The pious Israelites told of a Sabbatic River that flowed six days and rested on the seventh.[2] Josephus[3] makes this river flow only on the Sabbath day. The rabbis even taught that the damned in Gehenna had rest from torture on the Sabbath day.[4] They drew up a catalogue of thirty-nine principal works with many subdivisions under each, for which the penalty for violation was stoning. The Pharisaic wrath toward Jesus on this score was like a pent-up Utica, and blazed forth like a volcano of fury.

It is not perfectly clear how to relate the two next incidents in the Synoptic Gospels with that in John v., though they probably follow immediately.[5] If so, it is quite possible that some of the Jerusalem Pharisees followed Jesus back to Galilee in blind rage to see if they cannot find further proof against Him. Either

---

[1] *Shem.* R. xxx.; cf. also Philo, *Alleg.*, i. p. 46 (M.).
[2] Lightfoot, ii. p. 416.
[3] *War*, vii. 5, 1.
[4] Smith, *In the Days of His Flesh*, p. 131. See also Schuerer, *Jewish People*, div. ii. vol. ii. pp. 96-105.
[5] See Broadus' *Harmony of the Gospels*, pp. 41 ff.

this is true or the Pharisees in Galilee burst into spontaneous indignation against Jesus, perhaps after hearing of the incident in Jerusalem (John v.). The occasion of the complaint about plucking and eating heads of wheat on the Sabbath seems to us too trivial for reality, but the Talmud again reinforces the Gospels on this score, as we have already seen. The Pharisees regarded it as a most serious matter. The plucking of the heads of grain was reaping and rubbing the grain out was threshing, two kinds of labour on the Sabbath, of which the disciples had been guilty in the presence of Jesus and of the Pharisees. On this occasion Jesus took pains to make a prolonged argument on the subject in defence of the disciples and of Himself. He appealed to the example of David in eating the shew-bread (a case of necessity). He cited the conduct of the priests who work in the temple on the Sabbath, a conflict of duties where the higher prevails. He even claimed to be greater than the temple. He showed how Hosea interpreted God as preferring mercy to formal ritualistic sacrifice, a plea for works of mercy. He asserted His lordship as the Son of man over the Sabbath, with the right to make His own rules for its observance as opposed to those of the Pharisees. Jesus maintained that the Sabbath was made for the blessing of man, not for his bondage. Hence the day must be interpreted and observed in view of man's spiritual and physical welfare. This view of Jesus is one of the commonplaces of modern life. Indeed, to many who are used to the absolute license of modern continental Europe, reproduced, alas! in America, the views of Jesus seem needlessly strict, and even narrow, for they wish no restrictions of any kind, but a day of pleasure and revelry without any regard to man's moral and spiritual well-being.

On another Sabbath, possibly the next (these three Sabbaths may even come in succession), Jesus is in a synagogue in Galilee, and this time 'the scribes and Pharisees watched (παρετηροῦντο, descriptive imperfect, with an air of expectancy) him, whether he would heal on the Sabbath : that they might find how to accuse him' (Luke vi. 7). There we have the whole story in a nutshell. The Pharisees have now come to look for these Sabbath healings, a number of which Luke records (being a physician). 'Spies,' Plummer (on Luke vi. 7) calls them, who are here ready for any emergency and anxious to make a case against Jesus that will stand. Perhaps they looked sideways (παρά) out of the corner of their eyes. Matthew (xii. 10) adds that they finally asked : 'Is it lawful to heal on the Sabbath day ?' Thus they made a formal challenge before Jesus healed the man with the withered hand. Jesus accepted the challenge, made the man stand forth before them all, demanded whether it was 'lawful' (their very word) to do good or harm on the Sabbath, to save life or to kill it (they were at that moment full of murderous thoughts towards Jesus), 'looked round on them with anger' (Mark iii. 5) in righteous indignation at their perversity, and then made the man stretch forth his hand healed and whole right before the Pharisees. It was an intolerable affront to their dignity as well as one more violation of their rules. They stalked out of the synagogue in a towering rage ('filled with madness,' Luke vi. 11), and straightway conferred with the Herodians, whom they despised, in sheer desperation to find some way to destroy Jesus.

The next scene of this nature is pitched in Jerusalem again (John ix.), and is a rich and racy narrative of pith and humour. The Pharisees are unable to untie their own theological knot, quite of a piece with those so finely twisted in the Talmud. If Jesus were of God, He would not have healed the blind man on the Sabbath. And yet the man was healed on the Sabbath. Finally, they are willing to agree that he was healed on the Sabbath, provided the blind man will agree that the glory belongs to God, and that Jesus is a sinner for doing what adds glory to God and makes Jesus a sinner. The blind man has merry sport over the dilemma of the Pharisees, who in a rage turn on him: 'Thou wast altogether born in sins, and dost thou teach us? And they cast him out.'

In Judea (probably) Luke (xiii. 10-21) describes the pathetic case of the hunch-backed old woman, whom Jesus made a point of healing on the Sabbath in a synagogue. The ruler of the synagogue flew into a passion over this desecration of his synagogue, by such unholy deeds as healing the old woman instead of observing the Pharisaic ritual of worship. It was as undecorous as a soul's conversion would be in some churches under some sermons. The rebuke of the ruler by Jesus is withering in its irony and sarcasm.

Probably in Perea Jesus was invited by a Pharisee to dine (breakfast) and the Pharisees 'were watching him' (ἦσαν παρατηρούμενοι, Luke xiv. 1), according to custom, even though His host was a Pharisee. But Jesus took the initiative, challenged them for an attack, healed a man of the dropsy, and told them stories in illustration of the attitude of the host and the guests. Jesus was complete master of the occasion. But all these Sabbath controversies rankled in the hearts of the Pharisees.

(7) *Utterly Inadequate Signs* (Matt. xii. 38-45; xvi. 1; Mark viii. 11; Luke xi. 16-32)

Men to-day are troubled by the wealth of miracles attributed to Jesus, not by the paucity of them. Our scientific scruples call for a minimum of the supernatural. But the Pharisees were not content with the splendour of the signs wrought by Jesus. Jesus represents Abraham as saying to Lazarus in the parable : ' If they hear not Moses and the prophets, neither will they be persuaded, though one rise from the dead ' (Luke xvi. 31). The miracles of Jesus did induce belief in the claims of Jesus, and some of the multitude asked : ' When the Christ shall come, will he do more signs than this man hath done ? ' (John vii 31). But the Pharisees, when they heard the multitude murmuring these things concerning Jesus, sent officers to take Him. The raising of Lazarus from the dead persuaded many to believe in Jesus, but the scribes and Pharisees simply determined to put both Jesus and Lazarus to death (John xi. 45-53 ; xii. 9-11). The Pharisees had preconceived ideas as to how the Messiah was to come with supernatural manifestations from heaven. Satan, as already noted, seems to appeal to this popular Pharisaic theology when he proposed that Jesus be seen falling from the pinnacle of the temple as if dropping out of heaven (Matt. iv. 6 ; Luke iv. 9 f.). We see the Pharisees repeatedly coming to Jesus, and demanding a sign in spite of the multitude wrought by Him. ' Master, we would see a sign from thee ' (Matt. xii. 38), as if He were a miracle monger. They were too particular in their tastes for signs, and Jesus would give them only the sign of Jonah, His resurrection from the dead. Even after the feeding of the five thousand the Galilean crowd the next day in the synagogue say : ' What then doest thou for a sign, that we may see, and believe thee ? What workest thou ? ' (John vi. 30). They even suggested something on the scale of the manna in the days of Moses. They had punctilious ideas even about miracles, and were hard to please, these miracle tasters. Finally the Pharisees demand ' a sign from heaven ' (Matt. xvi. 1 ; Mark viii. 11), ' tempting him.' On this occasion the religious authorities (Pharisees, Sadducees, Herodians) combined against Jesus, as they had done against John the Baptist. But they do it under the guise of a friendly inquiry. They make the point (Plummer on Matt.) that the miracles of Jesus were on earth. Assuming that He is the Messiah, He must, according to Pharisaic theology, adduce signs in the heavens and from the heavens, if He wishes to satisfy popular expectation and be hailed as Messiah with proper credentials. It is no wonder that Mark (viii. 12) adds that 'he sighed deeply in his spirit.' This obstinate stupidity caused a sigh to come up ($\dot{a}\nu a\sigma\tau\epsilon\nu\acute{a}\xi as$) from the very depths of His soul. But they were familiar with the Bath Qol (Swete), and even the ministry of Elijah had heavenly attestation (1 Kings xviii. 38; 2 Kings i. 10 ff.). It is not certain whether the similar request for a sign in Luke xi. 16-32 is different from the incident in Matthew and Mark or not. It is not intrinsically improbable that in Perea, as in Galilee, the Pharisees should press this point against Jesus. Indeed, Jesus Himself said that at His second coming for judgment, the eschatological aspect of His reign, they would see 'the sign of the Son of Man in heaven : and then shall all the tribes of the earth mourn, and they shall see the Son of Man coming on the clouds of heaven with power and great glory' (Matt. xxiv. 30). But that 'sign' is not to be had as proof of His Messianic mission. When the Pharisees and Sadducees have Jesus on trial before the Sanhedrin, He boldly defied Caiaphas and all the rest and said : 'Henceforth ye shall see the Son of Man sitting at the right hand of power, and coming on the clouds of heaven' (Matt. xxvi. 64 ; Mark xiv. 62). Then Jesus will be the Judge of the Sanhedrin who are now judging Him. Then they shall have the sign from heaven which they so eagerly clamoured for while on earth.

(8) *Insolent Defiance of Tradition* (Matt. xv. 1-30; Mark vii. 1-23; Luke xi. 37-54)

Perhaps in no single incident do we see the contrast between the Pharisees and Jesus to better advantage than in the first conflict over the necessity of washing the hands before meals. M'Neile (Matt. *in loco*) thinks that the attack was made in Judea 'where the points at issue between the Rabbinic schools would be more likely to be brought up for discussion than in the north.' But Swete (Mark *in loco*) rightly observes that the Pharisees from Jerusalem have already (Mark iii. 22) been seen in Galilee, watching the teaching of Jesus. Swete also suggests that the opportunity for the disciples to eat bread with 'defiled' or common and unclean hands arose during the passage through the plain of Gennesaret after returning from the feeding of the five thousand the afternoon before (Mark vi. 45-56). The disciples had had a stormy night, and were hungry, and may have eaten of the twelve baskets full which they had preserved (Mark vi. 43). The Pharisees would be quick to notice this lapse from ceremonial purity and challenge Jesus with 'their old policy of insidious questioning' (Swete). Other instances of attack by questions are worth noting. This method was pursued by the Pharisees in regard to the failure of the disciples to fast (Mark ii. 18). So also by question they challenge His conduct and that of the disciples in the matter of Sabbath observance (Mark ii. 24; Matt. xii. 10). It was thus that the Pharisees attacked Jesus with the problem of divorce, 'tempting him and saying, 'Is it lawful for a man to put away his wife for every cause?'' (Matt. xix. 3, cf. Mark x. 2). On this subject also the schools of Hillel and Shammai took opposite views. The hope here was to inveigle Jesus into a position that would injure His popularity, not to obtain a charge against Him. In the series of queries on the last Tuesday of Christ's ministry a similar course is pursued. First the Sanhedrin (probably representatives) ask for His authority for His conduct in the temple. Then the Pharisees send some of their brightest disciples to 'catch him in his talk' (Mark xii. 13), and these raise the dilemma about tribute to Cæsar, hoping to entrap Him in treason to Cæsar, or to make Him unpopular with the people. The Sadducees next ask about the resurrection, with one of their stock conundrums on the subject which had discomfited the Pharisees. Then a lawyer in a formal way inquires about the great commandment of the law. This was a favourite method with the rabbis in their academic discussions, as we see abundantly illustrated in the Talmud. But it was more than academic as used by the Pharisees with Jesus, though M'Neile (Matt. xv. 12) holds that Jesus is treated as 'the leader of a Rabbinic "School," who might have a right to his opinion on a detail of "tradition."' Probably so as to the form in which the query is raised, but not in the spirit that prompts the 'tempting' so often mentioned. Buchler [1] holds that the Pharisees who attack Jesus about His disciples eating with unwashed hands must have been priests who had recently joined the ranks of the Pharisees, because of the strict views advanced about these rules of purification, designed to safeguard levitical purity, since the rabbis expounded these laws, but did not observe them. But these rules for those not priests probably arose from a practice already going on.[2] It is probable (M'Neile) that we are not to press Mark's words (vii. 3) too far: 'For the Pharisees, and all the Jews, except they wash their hands diligently, eat not, holding the traditions of the elders.' Certainly the 'Jews' who 'all' cherish 'the

---

[1] *Exp. Times*, xxi. pp. 34-40.
[2] Margoliouth, *Exp. Times*, xxii. pp. 261 ff.

tradition of the Elders are not the masses, but the strict and orthodox minority who supported the Scribes' (Swete). The mass of the common people probably did not know these details, and yet religious purification was found in religious households (Westcott on John ii. 6). Jesus may have been used to it in His own home as Peter had been (Acts x. 14). Jesus does not here resist the custom, but the effort to make it essential (Hort, *Judaistic Christianity*, pp. 29 f.). The Pharisees probably endeavoured to force their notions of cleanness upon all who would accept them, and had contempt for the common herd who knew not the law and did not care about these pious punctilios. Twelve treatises in the Mishna are devoted to the complicated amplifications of the rules for ceremonial purity which tradition had added to the law. We have seen already that the rabbis placed tradition (oral law) above the written law, and claimed Divine origin for it. Rabbi Aqibah used to say: 'Tradition is a fence to Torah.'[1] In this instance it is *Halachah*, not *Haggadah*, and Mark rightly presents the question of the Pharisees: 'Why *walk not* (οὐ περιπατοῦσιν like הִלְּכָה) thy disciples according to the tradition of the elders?' It is not a light matter of opinion, but a serious point of conduct that is raised. Montefiore thinks that the practice of washing hands 'was only instituted by Hillel and Shammai,' and hence (quoted by M'Neile) argues that there could have been no 'tradition' on the subject. But the custom probably antedated the teaching. One instance of the dispute between the schools of Hillel and Shammai on the subject occurs in the Mishna:[2] 'If any one places vessels under the pipes (which ran into the plunging bath), they make the bath unsuitable

---

[1] *Pirké Aboth*, iii. 20.
[2] *Mikwaoth*, iv. 1. See also Schuerer, *History of Jewish People*, div. ii. vol. ii. p. 110.

(because it then counts as drawn water). According to the school of Shammai, it is all the same, whether they have been placed there or forgotten; according to the school of Hillel, they do not make it unfit, if they were only forgotten.' The disputes on these rules of ceremonial cleansing added by the elders were only on petty details of a pettifogging nature. But Jesus was not to be caught in this net of minutiæ. He turned upon them with vehemence and keen irony for their whole miserable attitude of subordinating the commandment of God to tradition: 'Full well do ye reject the commandment of God that ye may keep your tradition.' They would probably have admitted the charge and even gloried in it. When the commandment (ἐντολή) and tradition (παράδοσις) clashed, tradition was supreme (M'Neile), because the written law was originally oral, and this fact gave the oral law precedence (Plummer on Matt.).[1] The meaning of corban we shall leave to the next chapter, the discussion of Christ's indictment of the Pharisees. Jesus here stung the Pharisees with the word 'hypocrites.'

Luke (xi. 37-54) records the invitation of Jesus to breakfast from a Pharisee (probably in Judea), which was not a plot to get evidence against Him, since he seems to have been taken by surprise that Jesus had not bathed (his hands, at any rate) before the meal (Plummer *in loco*). The Pharisees had evidently expected Jesus to conform to Pharisaic custom, since He was a guest in the Pharisee's house, and had been with the crowds and was unclean from the Pharisee's standpoint. It must be kept in mind that the objection of the Pharisees was not on grounds of hygiene. They were not familiar with the germ theory of disease. Plummer thinks that Jesus, knowing that the Pharisees laid so much stress on the necessity of ceremonial purity

[1] Cf. 'Law' in Hastings' *D.B.*, and 'Tradition' in Hastings' *D.C.G.*

II.] PHARISAIC RESENTMENT TOWARD JESUS 97

in connection with meals, purposely abstained, as a protest against these trivial rules. That is possible, but it is also conceivable that Jesus meant to make no point of the matter at all till the Pharisees manifested such intense amazement at Christ's lack of scrupulosity in the matter. Edersheim [1] gives a picture of the etiquette at a feast as given in the Talmud.[2] 'As the guests enter, they sit down in chairs, and water is brought to them, with which they wash one hand. After this the cup is taken, when each speaks the blessing over the wine partaken of before dinner. Presently they all lie down at table. Water is again brought them, with which they now wash both hands, preparatory to the meal, when the blessing is spoken over the bread, and then over the cup, by the chief person at the feast, or else by one selected by way of distinction.' Probably at this breakfast the ceremonies had not proceeded very far before the clash came. It is interesting to note what sticklers people are for table manners, which vary in all ages and lands, but which are considered marks of good breeding. The Pharisees bluntly thought Jesus ill-bred, and undoubtedly showed it in a way that brought embarrassment all round. The severe reply of Jesus (to be discussed later) thus had sufficient occasion.

(9) *An Ignorant Impostor* (John vii. 14-30 ; Matt. xxvii. 63 f.)

This attitude toward Jesus is implied in all the charges made, but it comes out with clearness during Christ's visit to the feast of tabernacles six months before His death. It is reflected in the criticism of a portion of the Galilean multitude before Jesus comes to the feast, who said in reply to the defence of those who called Him 'a

[1] *Life and Times*, vol. ii. p. 207.
[2] *Ber.* 43a.

good man' these blunt words: 'Nay, but He leads the multitude astray' (οὔ, ἀλλὰ πλανᾷ τὸν ὄχλον, John vii. 12). In spite of all that the Pharisees had done Jesus was still a popular idol with many in Galilee. The Pharisees 'marvelled at this strange success, while they did not admit His irregular claims' (Westcott on John vii. 15). The people who followed the Pharisees rather than Jesus accepted their interpretation of His success. He was merely a 'self-taught enthusiast' without real culture, without credentials, without moral convictions, without spiritual power. The secret of His apparent success lay in the gullibility of the ignorant populace. This is the explanation of the temporary success of many a pretender beyond a doubt. False prophets (Zech. xiii. 2) had already arisen in plenty. It was common enough for false claimants for the throne to appear. Josephus [1] tells how in the disorders during the rule of Archelaus one man, Athronges, an ignorant man with no claim by descent or culture or power, 'yet because he was a tall man, and excelled others in the strength of his hands, he was so bold as to set up for king.' The Pharisee Gamaliel actually reminded the Sanhedrin of the fate that befell Theudas and Judas of Galilee, in their false claims to be 'somebody,' as a reason for patience with the apostles of Jesus. Let God and time deal with them (Acts v. 33-42). Jesus will warn the disciples of 'false Christs' (ψευδόχριστοι) who will come and lead astray if possible, even the elect, by saying: 'I am the Christ,' or 'Lo, here is the Christ; or, Lo, there' (Matt. xxiv. 5, 23 f.; Mark xiii. 21 f.). It is even probable that some of the leaders of the Zealot revolts had already claimed to be Messiahs. Certainly some 'persuaded the multitude to follow them into the wilderness, and pretended that they would manifest wonders and signs, that should be performed

[1] *Ant.*, bk. xvii. ch. x. § 7.

PHARISAIC RESENTMENT TOWARD JESUS

by the providence of God' (Jos., *Ant.*, xx. viii. 6). H. M. Hughes (*Exp. Times*, Jan. 1916) suggests that Barabbas was one of these Zealots who laid claims to being a political Messiah There seems proof of Zealot activity from the N. T. itself. Cf. the Galileans slain by Pilate (Luke xiii. 1), the Egyptian the assassin in Acts xxi. 38 The Assumption of Moses (7-30 A.D.) is decidedly anti-Zealot. Josephus calls the Zealots 'robbers.' False claimants will make use of the name of Jesus.[1] In our own day we have seen two men claim to be the Messiah, and one woman set herself above Jesus as the revealer of God. The masses of the Jews welcomed each hero as he appeared,[2] John, Jesus, or Bar-Cochba (the son of a star). Curiously enough the great Rabbi Aqiba in his old age, during the reign of Hadrian, threw himself into the camp of the Messianic Pretender, Bar-Cochab (Barcochba), when he appeared before the Sanhedrin. The Sanhedrin condemned Jesus as a blasphemer for claiming to be the Messiah, and hailed with joy this wild enthusiast because he raised the standard of revolt against Rome. Aqiba said to the listening people : ' Behold, the Star that is come out of Jacob ; the days of redemption are at hand.' Aqiba died a martyr to this 'ignoble cause.'[3] If Jesus had only dared to raise the standard of revolt against Rome, the Pharisees would have hailed Him with joy as Messiah. But they had no patience with a merely spiritual Messiah who left the Jewish nation under the Roman yoke. The Pharisees evince a fine literary scorn for Jesus, in spite of His skill in debate and power as a teacher. ' How knoweth this man letters, having never learned?' (John vii. 15). He is bound to be ignorant, since he had not studied in either of the two

---

[1] Heitmüller, *Im Namen Jesu*, p. 63.
[2] Volz, *Jud. Eschatologie*, p. 209.
[3] Pick, *What is the Talmud?* p. 40.

great theological schools in Jerusalem (Hillel and Shammai). The marvellous acumen and clarity of His thought counted as nothing with the Pharisees, for it did not bear their stamp. Since He did not go to their schools, He had simply taught Himself. Therefore His opinions had no scholarly weight. They were supported by no great rabbis of the past. He was not worth listening to. Jesus admits the fact of His lack of Pharisaic training, but denies the conclusion that He originated His ideas. There is a peril in all self-taught men, the danger of conceit and over-emphasis upon their own originality, because of lack of contact with the great minds of all ages. Jesus sees that and claims God as the source of His teaching, and suggests how the Pharisees can put to the test this claim for His teaching. Doing the will of God will qualify one to judge of God's teaching (John vii. 17). It is sound psychology. Those who bring their wills in harmony with God's will are competent to pass on the character of God's teaching, and so of Christ's claims (Westcott *in loco*). Rabban Gamaliel (*Aboth*, ii. 4) is quoted in the Talmud as saying : ' Do His will as if it were thy will, that He may do thy will as if it were His will.' The Pharisees made no reply to this defence of Jesus, but they reveal their attitude of scorn when the officers sent to arrest Jesus return without Him : ' Are ye also led astray ? ' (John vii. 47). None of the rulers of the Pharisees had believed on the upstart from Galilee. The accursed ignorant multitude did not count. They could hardly believe that the Roman soldiers had fallen victims to the spell of the deceiver.

One of the charges made against Jesus was, that He bore witness of Himself, and hence it was not true (John viii. 13). Jesus had recognised the need of witness outside of Himself and had offered it (John v. 31 ff.). But He contends for His right to testify concerning

Himself, and He tells the truth even if these Pharisees refuse to accept it (John viii. 14). Nevertheless He appeals to the witness of His Father, whereupon the Pharisees imply that He is a bastard : ' Where is thy Father ? ' (viii. 19). We have seen that in the Talmud it is repeatedly asserted that Jesus was the son of a paramour of Mary.

Matthew (xxvii. 62-6) records the precaution of the chief priests and the Pharisees, to have the Roman seal placed on the tomb of Jesus, and a Roman guard stationed to watch over it. They said to Pilate : ' Sir, we remember that that deceiver said ' (ἐκεῖνος ὁ πλάνος εἶπεν). They would not call His name to Pilate, but they fear Him though dead, and would like for ' that deceiver ' to be His epitaph. Their contempt for Jesus was shown to the man born blind (John ix. 29) by saying : ' But as for this man, we know not whence he is,' an unknown upstart of a nobody. But with all their pride of victory they are afraid that ' the last error (ἡ ἐσχάτη πλάνη) will be worse than the first' (Matt. xxvii. 64). The first error (πλάνη) about the deceiver (πλάνος) was to accept Him as Messiah. The second will be to believe in His resurrection. The Pharisees had more ground for their fear than they knew. ' That deceiver ' did rise from the dead, and ' the last error ' has revealed the hollow emptiness of the Pharisaism that killed Him, and has become the acme and goal of truth for all the race with Pharisaism as the dead husk. Justin Martyr (Dial. 108) charges the Jews with describing Christianity thus : ' A certain godless and lawless sect (heresy) has arisen from one Jesus, a Galilean deceiver.'[1]

Herford (*Pharisaism*, p. 143) says that it was ' inevitable that they should regard him as a dangerous heretic.' They surely did. It is pleasing to note a

---

[1] Αἱρεσίς τις ἄθεος καὶ ἄνομος ἐγήγερται ἀπὸ 'Ιησοῦ τινος Γαλιλαίου πλάνου.

more kindly temper toward Jesus by the modern liberal Jews, like Montefiore, who gladly acclaim Jesus as one of the greatest of Jewish prophets, and who advocate a study of the New Testament, but this new temper does not alter the historical situation in the first century. W. J. Sparrow-Simpson ('Liberal Judaism and the Christian Faith,' *Quarterly Review* for October 1915) calls this new attitude of reformed Jews toward Jesus 'a revolution of the first magnitude,' but the problem of the person of Jesus is evaded.

(10) *Plotting to Destroy the Temple* (John ii. 19-22; Matt. xxvi. 61; Mark xiv. 58; Matt. xxvii. 39 f.; Mark xv. 29)

When the Pharisees first challenged the authority of Jesus, He gave the sign of His resurrection in symbolic language—'Destroy this temple, and in three days I will raise it up' (John ii. 19)—that they did not understand nor did the disciples then. It was treasured against Him as a threat against the temple. The Jews had been very suspicious about the work of Herod the Great on the temple, and only allowed him to change it a piece at a time. He began it about B.C. 19, and died B.C. 4, and the temple was not yet finished A.D. 27. It was a fresh ground of distrust when these words were turned against Jesus at His trial. It was a sort of last resort, to be sure, after other lines of attack before the Sanhedrin had failed. The Sanhedrin had brought Jesus before the court without an indictment and with no witnesses. They were to be the judges of His case, and yet 'the whole council sought witness against Jesus to put Him to death' (Mark xiv. 55), 'false witness' Matthew (xxvi. 59) adds, 'and they found it not, though many false witnesses came' (xxvi. 60). The Pharisees share with the Sadducees the responsibility for the legal

II.]   PHARISAIC RESENTMENT TOWARD JESUS   103

irregularities connected with the trial of Jesus before the Sanhedrin, in spite of modern efforts to blame the Sadducees for the whole proceeding. Montefiore [1] pictures Jesus going to Jerusalem 'bearding the Sadducean priesthood and the antagonistic high authorities in their very den.' But the Pharisees cannot escape their leadership from the start, and that finally enlisted the Sadducees against the common enemy of corrupt Judaism. This is not the place for detailed discussion of the illegalities in the trial of Jesus. They have received ample treatment at the hands of skilled lawyers.[2] It is pitiful special pleading when Rabbi Drucker [3] endeavours to show that conspiracy of the high priest turned Jesus over to Pilate against the wishes of the Pharisees and the Jewish people who hailed Him as a hero. He argues that the illegalities shown in the Gospels prove that the trial before the Sanhedrin did not take place. He professes to show this 'from Jewish sources,' but it is all *a priori* and unconvincing. The false witnesses, probably suborned as in the charges against Stephen (Acts vi. 11), failed to agree and misrepresented what Jesus had said : ' I am able to destroy the temple of God, and to build it in three days.' The case fell through as it stood, but this charge was hurled in the teeth of Jesus by the wagging crowds who passed along the highway as Jesus hung on the cross : ' Ha ! thou that destroyest the temple, and buildest it in three days, save thyself and come down from the cross ' (Mark xv. 30). It is hard to stop a slander, once it is started. Hired false witnesses will one day testify against Stephen : ' For we have heard him say that this Jesus of Nazareth shall destroy this place, and shall change the customs which Moses delivered unto us '

---

[1] *The Religious Teaching of Jesus*, p. 134.
[2] Like Chapman, Chandler, Greenleaf, Innes, Wilson.
[3] *The Trial of Jesus*.

(Acts vi. 14). Herford (*Pharisaism*, p. 127) says 'That the Pharisees knew why they distrusted, feared, and finally helped to destroy Jesus is plain enough.' The reasons that they gave seem to us wholly inadequate, but at bottom they felt that they had to destroy Jesus or be destroyed by Him. It was a sort of primal instinct which they could not clearly analyse. It comes out in the meeting of the chief priests and the Pharisees after the raising of Lazarus : 'If we let him thus alone, all men will believe on him : and the Romans will come and take away both our place and our nation' (John xi. 48). This is a remarkable confession for candour in putting 'place' before 'nation,' pocket before patriotism. Westcott (*in loco*) puts it mildly thus : 'They look at the hypothetical catastrophe from its personal side as affecting themselves.' It is pertinent to add that they did kill Jesus, and all the same as a punishment therefor, as Jesus later predicted (Matt. xxi. 43), the Romans in A.D. 70 came and took away both their place and their nation. The temple whose fate Jesus foresaw, because Jerusalem had rejected Him, was destroyed, but not at the hands of Jesus. The customs of Moses and the traditions of the elders were preserved by the Pharisees, who came to dominate the life of Judaism. But in the struggle between Christianity and Rabbinism in the thought and life of the world Rabbinism has been hopelessly outdistanced by the power of the very Jesus whom they rejected, and thought that they had destroyed.

(11) *High Treason against Cæsar* (Luke xxiii. 2 ; John xviii. 8-30–xix. 15 ; Luke xxiii. ; Matt. xxvii. 17-25 ; Mark xv. 9-14)

The Sanhedrin did not at this juncture have the power of life and death (John xviii. 31) and were not willing

to relieve Pilate of His responsibility in the case, for
they wished the death of Jesus, not His punishment,
still less His acquittal. It is significant that the Sanhedrin failed to inform Pilate that they had already tried
Jesus, and had condemned Him to death on the charge
of blasphemy. Instead of asking him to endorse their
action, they remained silent on the whole subject, and
brought the case to Pilate as a new action. One is at
a loss to understand why they took the trouble to have
the ecclesiastical trial, since they knew that it was
useless after all. Perhaps they did it as a relief to their
own feelings of exasperated indignation, shown in their
conduct after the vote when some of the members of
the Sanhedrin spat in the face of Jesus, blindfolded
Him, buffeted Him, mocked Him, and said: 'Prophesy
unto us, thou Christ, who is he that struck thee' (Matt.
xxvi. 67 f.; Mark xiv. 65; Luke xxii. 63-5). Perhaps
also the Sanhedrin wished to go through the form of the
trial as a protest to the loss of real power at the hands
of the Romans. At any rate, they seem to be more at
ease in making charges before Pilate, than they had
been in securing witnesses against Jesus before the
Sanhedrin. With all their malevolence, it was only the
confession of Jesus that supplied the Sanhedrin with
the technical charge of blasphemy when all other charges
had fallen through for lack of evidence. But they bring
a political accusation before Pilate, for he would consider
none of their theological verbosities any more than
Gallio would in the charges against Paul in Corinth
(Acts xviii. 12-16). The Sanhedrin 'began to accuse'
(Luke xxiii. 2) Jesus with three accusations (sedition,
forbidding to give tribute to Cæsar, assuming the title
of king), but they were all of a piece, and doubtless the
'many things' mentioned later (Matt. xxvii. 13; Mark
xv. 3) were simply expansions of these three. The
charge of sedition or 'perverting' ($\delta\iota\alpha\sigma\tau\rho\acute{\epsilon}\phi o\nu\tau\alpha$) the

Jewish nation was a matter of opinion, but a specious one, because of the great excitement caused by the ministry of Jesus. In particular, the Triumphal Entry was a striking instance. But the Pharisees knew perfectly well that Jesus had discouraged any effort that hinted at insurrection (John vi. 14 f.). He had in plain words advocated giving tribute to Cæsar (Luke xx. 35) when the Pharisees and Herodians endeavoured to catch Him with this question a few days before. These two charges were simply made to prepare for the third and really serious one : 'We found this man' (τοῦτον εὕραμεν), as if caught in the very act by the zealous friends of Rome (the Pharisees) in their eager search to uphold Roman rights, 'saying that he is Christ a king' (λέγοντα ἑαυτὸν χριστὸν βασιλέα εἶναι). Here they do use the term 'Messiah' or 'Christ,' for claiming which title the Sanhedrin had already condemned Jesus for blasphemy, but they added 'a king,' by way of definition, in order to give a political complexion to the charge. The Sanhedrin knew that Pilate would be compelled to take notice of this charge, as he did. All Four Gospels record the question put by Pilate to Jesus within the palace as 'Jesus stood before the governor ' : 'Art thou the king of the Jews ?' (Matt. xxvii. 11 ; Mark xv. 2 ; Luke xxiii. 3 ; John xviii. 33). To make a claim like that was in reality high treason, the gravest crime against the state. The Synoptic Gospels all represent Jesus simply as confessing it in the words 'Thou sayest,' but John has a more extended report of the conversation between Jesus and Pilate, in which Jesus explains what He means by claiming to be king. 'My Kingdom is not of this world,' He said. 'To this end am I come into the world, that I may bear witness unto the truth.' The supercilious question of Pilate, 'What is truth ?' shows clearly that he saw no conflict between the unworldly realm of truth and the rule of

Cæsar. At best Jesus was a harmless enthusiast. Jesus had tried to explain that 'as a spiritual king He was open to no accusation of hostility to the empire' (Westcott). Pilate had discernment enough to see that, and went out and said to the Sanhedrin: 'I find no crime in him.'

But what shall we say of the motive and spirit of the Sanhedrin in making this accusation? To begin with, the Pharisees expected a political Messiah, who would set up a world empire and drive out the Romans. Later, as already noted, they rallied around Bar-Cochba in this very attempt. They did not consider it a heresy or a crime for the Messiah to claim to be a political king. Besides, they knew very well that Jesus did not pretend to be a political Messiah or an earthly king as a rival to Cæsar's rule. What Jesus had explained to Pilate was precisely what the Pharisees knew that Jesus taught about Himself. Indeed, it was the very refusal of Jesus to be a political Messiah of the Pharisaic type, and to lead in a revolt against the Romans, that angered them most of all. In their desperation, therefore, the Pharisees twist the words of Jesus about being 'Christ a king' (King Messiah) into meaning precisely the opposite of what they knew to be the truth. At first they leave Pilate to place his own construction on the words, knowing that, of course, he would take them in a political sense. But at last, in spite of all their chicanery, Pilate saw through their envy (Matt. xxvii. 18) and, impressed afresh by the personality of Jesus, was about to release Him even after having given formal consent to the crucifixion, because the Sanhedrin had in their moment of triumph tried to give a salve to the conscience of Pilate by explaining that by 'Messiah a king' Jesus 'made himself the Son of God' (John xix. 6-12). Thus the Sanhedrin had robbed the charge of its political colour and really had no case in Pilate's court, for he had no jurisdiction over ecclesiastical and theological disputes. True, Cæsar did receive divine worship as god, but Pilate was not disposed to champion that aspect of the matter, or to treat Jesus as a divine rival to Tiberius. The Jews were quick to see that they had made a terrible blunder, and sought to retrieve it by repeating the political charge with a direct threat to Pilate : 'If thou release this man, thou art not Cæsar's friend : every one that maketh himself a king speaketh against Cæsar' (John xix. 12). This was an appeal to Pilate's fears. The Sanhedrin knew that Pilate knew of his misrule, and that they would be able to make many charges against him. Pilate was more afraid of Tiberius than he was of Jesus. It mattered little that the charge against Jesus was untrue. Jesus had confessed to the use of the term 'King,' and Tiberius would not overlook Pilate's negligence on that subject. In order to carry their point the Sanhedrin actually posed as the special champions of Cæsar against Pilate, who was trying to shield the usurper Jesus. 'We have no king but Cæsar' (John xix. 15), the chief priests (Sadducees) answered this time, but the Pharisees let it pass. The Sadducees had already given up the Messianic hope, and had made peace with the world as it was. So now at the end of the day the Sadducees proclaim the abnegation of the Messianic hope and the Pharisees make no protest, so eager are they to put Jesus to death. 'They first rejected Jesus as the Christ, and then, driven by the irony of circumstances, they rejected the Christ altogether' (Westcott, John *in loco*). Jewish hate against Jesus had won. And yet the victory was worse than any defeat that the Jews ever had. It was indeed 'The Hebrew Tragedy' (Conder). Jesus came unto His own home-land ($\epsilon\dot{\iota}s$ $\tau\dot{\alpha}$ $\ddot{\iota}\delta\iota\alpha$) and His own people ($o\dot{\iota}$ $\ddot{\iota}\delta\iota o\iota$) received Him not. The legend of the Wandering Jew tells the sad story of the ceaseless round of this strange and wonderful race whose glory is that Jesus was a Jew, and for whom together with the Roman soldiers Jesus prayed as He hung upon the cross : ' Father, forgive them, for they know not what they do ' (Luke xxiii. 34).

CHAPTER III

THE CONDEMNATION OF THE PHARISEES BY JESUS

THE peril of Pharisaism in Christianity is the emphasis on the letter as opposed to the spirit. The letter killeth while the spirit quickeneth. It is sometimes charged that the words of Jesus to the Pharisees are unduly harsh, and not in accord with His own teaching on the subject of captious criticism (Matt. vii. 1 f.; Luke vi. 37 f.). But is the criticism of Jesus captious? It is plain and pointed beyond a doubt and not without a sting at times. But one must consider the provocation that elicited such words from our Lord, and the prolonged restraint on His part under the severe taunts of His enemies. Those who should have welcomed Jesus and His message were the chief opponents in His path. It became necessary for Jesus to reveal these religious leaders in their true character in order that the people might understand both them and Jesus, and the reason for the conflict between them. Religious controversy is a calamity, but it is often unavoidable, unless one is willing to give error a clear road to victory. Loyalty to truth demands that one speak the truth in love for those in error. It must not be forgotten that Jesus is the one under attack, and that his descriptions of the Pharisees are in the nature of self-defence. I am not seeking to mitigate the severity of the language or to soften it of its true import. The hot hatred of the Pharisees for Jesus did not beget hate in the heart of Jesus. He prayed for them as He died for them. And yet Jesus did not cover up the truth about them. His words about them are a judgment upon them for their spiritual and moral shortcomings. ' And this is the judgment, that the light is come into the world, and men loved the darkness rather than the light; for their works were evil' (John iii. 19). If these are not the words of Jesus, they are at least the Evangelist's estimate of the reason why the Jerusalem leaders rejected Jesus. At bottom, the reason that men refuse Christ is always the love of sin. The presence of Jesus sharpened the sense of spiritual reality. The issue is drawn and the tug of war is on. Sin pulls hard upon even the respectable religious classes, though often in the guise of piety, selfish religiosity. At any rate, there is nothing to conceal in what Jesus has said to the Pharisees, but much to enlighten us and all who are in like peril with them. One's very virtues may become vices to deaden spiritual life.

1. *Spiritual Blindness* (John iii. 1-14 ; Matt. ix. 13 ; Luke v. 39 ; Mark iii. 5 ; Matt. xiii. 13-17 ; Mark iv. 12 ; Luke viii. 10 ; John vi. 44, 64 f. ; Matt. xv. 12-20 ; Matt. xvi. 1-4 ; Mark viii. 11-13 ; John ix. 40 f. ; Luke xi. 37-54)

It is remarkable that the first formal interview between Jesus and a friendly Pharisee reveals such a gulf between them. The difficulty that Nicodemus had in understanding Jesus' teaching about the kingdom of God, argues strongly against the view that Jesus had only the theological outlook of the Pharisees and the apocalyptists of His day. Dr. Kirsopp Lake [1] sees clearly that to hold this view robs Jesus of His place as infallible guide, not to say Lord and Saviour. 'It is

[1] *The Stewardship of Faith*, p. 51.

impossible to find its fulfilment in Jesus, if He conditioned His teaching by Jewish apocalypticism, and believed in what was, after all, an illusory expectation of the coming of the kingdom of God.' Dr. Lake [1] gives up Jesus, because he simply fell in with Jewish apocalypticism. 'We are driven back to a living religion of communion with God, without the intervention of any other guide claiming to be an infallible substitute for personal effort.' Dr. Lake, like Dr. Case,[2] offers by way of consolation the personal religion of Jesus rather than Jesus as religion. Jesus did make use of apocalyptic terminology in some of His teaching in order to be understood, but it is lamentable narrowness of view to see only this aspect of His teaching. Nicodemus is a cultured Pharisee and member of the Sanhedrin, who is drawn to Jesus by the nobility of His teaching and by the seal of God in the miracles of Jesus, as 'a teacher come from God' (John iii. 2). Jesus saw the fundamental trouble at once, and proceeded to explain to Nicodemus how one must be born again to enter the kingdom of God. Nicodemus probably looked for a political kingdom and a political Messiah, who would usher in the kingdom with catastrophic signs from heaven, but he was helpless to grasp the idea of a spiritual birth in a spiritual realm. The repeated effort of Jesus to make it plain to Nicodemus by means of the symbol of water and the necessity affirmed without the symbol, left Nicodemus in a state of scientific and theological scepticism. 'How can these things be?' (John iii. 9). There was probably no Pharisee in Jerusalem more enlightened than Nicodemus, but he was in the grip of Torah, and felt that there was an incompatibility somewhere, though he could not explain it. 'Torah and Jesus could not remain in harmony. The two were

[1] *The Stewardship of Faith*, p. 52.
[2] *The Historicity of Jesus*; *The Evolution of Early Christianity*.

fundamentally incompatible.'[1] As a result of this *impasse* with Nicodemus, Jesus exclaimed, 'Art thou the teacher of Israel, and understandest not these things?' (John iii. 10).[2] The Greek article (ὁ) with teacher is to be noted. Nicodemus was one of the authorised exponents of current Pharisaism, the accepted teacher of religion, one supposed to know by experience (γινώσκεις) the difficult points of theology, and certainly the more elementary. And yet he has shown ignorance of one of the fundamental matters, 'the earthly' (τὰ ἐπίγεια, taking place on earth). How can he be trusted to expound 'the heavenly' (τὰ ἐπουράνια, belonging to heaven as a sphere) like the plan of God in the Cross (the atonement) and the gift of His Son? There is no further comment by Nicodemus, and the incident apparently closes with Nicodemus unsaved. Later he did find his way to espouse the cause of Jesus, but he had to shake off much of the preconceived Pharisaic theology before he could understand or trust Jesus as the Revealer of God. Nicodemus thus stands as the representative Pharisee who is kindly disposed toward Jesus, and yet is hindered by the wealth of his own theology from finding a place for Him. He is the teacher who is blinded by his own knowledge. The light that is in him is darkness. Nicodemus was a sincere seeker after the truth, and Jesus treated him with consideration, as He does all scholars who make their way to Him. There is to-day many a scholar who has lost his way, and is unable to find God. I often think of Geo. J. Romanes as a modern Nicodemus, who fought his way out of doubt and darkness into light, truth, and peace.

It is probably nearly a year later that in Capernaum, at the feast of Levi, Jesus said to the Pharisees who

[1] Herford, *Pharisaism*, p. 146.
[2] Σὺ εἶ ὁ διδάσκαλος τοῦ Ἰσραὴλ καὶ ταῦτα οὐ γινώσκεις.

criticised His affiliation with publicans and sinners: 'But go ye and learn what this meaneth, I desire mercy and not sacrifice; for I came not to call the righteous, but sinners' (Matt. ix. 13). Here Jesus charges the rabbis with ignorance of Hosea vi. 6, a keen rebuke for the recognised preachers of the day. The 'go ye and learn' (πορευθέντες μάθετε) was a common formula with the rabbis (Plummer on Matt. ix. 13), and the use of it by Jesus as a rabbi to rabbis has additional force and even sting. The Pharisees had built up this system of ceremonial ritualism, because of ignorance of the inner spiritual teaching of the Old Testament itself. Lake [1] declines to see any irony in Christ's description of the Pharisees as 'the righteous,' but, as we have already seen, Lake limits the horizon of Jesus to His theological environment.

In Luke v. 39 Jesus gives a parable that helps to explain the obscurantism of the Pharisees, and their reluctance to accept the new theology of Jesus: 'And no man having drunk old wine desireth new: for he saith, The old is good.' [2] Wetstein curiously misunderstood the parable and took the Pharisaic austerity to be the new wine, and the teaching of Jesus the old wine,[3] just the reverse of the fact. As Plummer (*in loco*) clearly shows, it is not here the relative merits of the old wine and the new, but the *taste* for them that is under discussion. From the Pharisaic standpoint theirs is the old wine and the teaching of Jesus is the new wine. They not only prefer the old or 'good' (χρηστός, tried and known), but they will not even investigate the merits of the new, which has no attraction for them at all. Jesus thus clearly understands the Pharisaic attitude

---

[1] *The Stewardship of Faith*, p. 33.

[2] Οὐδεὶς πιὼν παλαιὸν θέλει νέον· λέγει γὰρ Ὁ παλαιὸς χρηστός ἐστιν. D and most of the Old Latin MSS. omit the verse.

[3] Pharisaeorum austeritas comparatur vino novo, Christi lenitas vino veteri.

III.] CONDEMNATION OF THE PHARISEES 115

toward His revolutionary teaching of a spiritual religion free from the bondage of rite and ceremony. Their minds are closed to His teaching, and they will not even investigate the matter as Nicodemus did. They refuse to consider the proposition that Jesus may be right and the Pharisees wrong. The case is prejudiced and closed to argument.

In Mark iii. 5 we have a vivid picture of the emotion of Jesus over the growing hostility of the Pharisees toward Him : 'And when He had looked round about on them with anger, being grieved at the hardening of their hearts.'[1] Mark has five instances of this 'quick, searching glance' of Jesus round the circle ($\pi\epsilon\rho\iota$-) of His friends or His enemies (Swete *in loco*), due probably to Peter's memory of the scenes. One of the looks at Peter cut him to the heart, and he went out and wept bitterly. The countenance of Jesus spoke volumes to those who saw Him.[2] The look of Jesus here was with anger, but it was not vindictive (Gould *in loco*), but anger tempered with grief (Swete). The sorrow ($\sigma\upsilon\nu$-$\lambda\upsilon\pi o\acute{\upsilon}\mu\epsilon\nu o\varsigma$) here is Christ's own misery over the hardness of heart of the Pharisees. 'The look was momentary, the sorrow habitual' (Swete). The Pharisees are now grown callous ($\pi\acute{\omega}\rho\omega\sigma\iota\varsigma$. Cf. the state of the heathen in Eph. iv. 18) as is shown directly by the plot with the Herodians to kill Him. Jesus did not express His look in words, nor did the Pharisees accept His challenge about the relative value of a man and a sheep. Instead, Jesus made the man stretch forth his withered hand. But the atmosphere of hostility was electric, and the tension was all the greater because no debate came. The Pharisees had looked their hate ($\pi\alpha\rho\epsilon\tau\eta$-$\rho o\hat{\upsilon}\nu\tau o$, were watching Him, Luke vi. 7) and Jesus in return had looked His anger

[1] Καὶ περιβλεψάμενος αὐτοὺς μετ' ὀργῆς, συνλυπούμενος ἐπὶ τῇ πωρώσει τῆς καρδίας αὐτῶν.
[2] Bengel, *Vultus Christi multa nos docuit.*

One of the severest indictments of the Pharisees for spiritual blindness occurs in the defence of Jesus for the extended use of parables (Matt. xiii. 13-17; Mark iv. 12; Luke viii. 10). It is after the blasphemous accusations and the disciples question Jesus about it: 'Why speakest thou unto them in parables?' (Matt. xiii. 10). Jesus says: 'Therefore speak I to them in parables; because seeing they see not, and hearing they hear not, neither do they understand.' He had just said that it was given to the believers to understand the mystery of the kindgom (Mark iv. 11), but His enemies no longer deserved the plain presentation of the message. The use of parables was for them a just penalty for their intellectual dullness and hardness of heart. In Mark and Luke the use of 'that' ($\mathit{\text{ἵνα}}$) rather than 'because' ($\mathit{\text{ὅτι}}$) has been urged as proof that Jesus purposely concealed the knowledge that He was the Messiah,[1] but the Greek particle ($\mathit{\text{ἵνα}}$) is sometimes used in the Koine for result. Still, the language of Isaiah quoted in Matt. xiii. 15 is negative purpose, 'lest haply they should perceive with their eyes, and understand with their hearts.' At any rate, in Matt. xiii. 14 Jesus interprets Isaiah vi. 9, 10, as fulfilled ($\mathit{\text{ἀναπληροῦται αὐτοῖς}}$, filling up full for them) in the case of the Pharisees. They were undergoing spiritual atrophy, so that they could not hear or see or understand. They were losing connection with the spiritual world. One of the new discoveries in optics is that the eye may function properly enough, but no image may be conveyed to the brain, because the special brain cell which keeps the record of like impressions has suddenly given way. One may be perfectly normal and rational about all else, and yet not be able to read at all, though seeing everything clearly enough except the letters of the alphabet, which are blurred into vacancy. In such

[1] J. Weiss, *Das älteste Evang.*, pp. 52-9.

CONDEMNATION OF THE PHARISEES

cases, one has to begin all over again and learn his alphabet. This is the charge that Jesus here makes against the Pharisees. They have lost the gift of spiritual sight or insight into spiritual things. Jesus speaks to them in an unknown tongue. They have lost the use of the ear, eye and heart. This is the law of nature and of grace. The failure to use an organ leads to the loss of the organ. The proper use of the organ develops the organ and enriches the user. The Pharisees were the heirs of the past, and had the privilege of witnessing the Messianic times which prophets of old (Moses, Isaiah, Micah) had desired to see (Matt. xiii. 17). And now, alas! the Pharisees stare at the wondrous sight with wide-open blind eyes, and the message of Jesus the Messiah falls upon ears deadened and dulled to the sweetest of all sounds. Their hearts are tough like the tanned hide of an animal no longer sensitive to life and truth. What a pitiful description! The Psalms of Solomon (a Pharisaic book) had said: 'Blessed are they that shall be born in those days, to behold the blessings of Israel' (xvii. 50). If the words of Jesus sound hard and pitiless, it must be noted that He is speaking as an interpreter of facts. The Pharisees had made their choice, and Jesus must go on with His task.

When Jesus denounced the Pharisees for making void the word of God by their tradition, the disciples, after they had gone into the house (Mark vii. 17), said: 'Knowest thou that the Pharisees were offended (caused to stumble, ἐσκανδαλίσθησαν) when they heard this saying?' (Matt. xv. 12). Evidently the Pharisees winced under the burning words of Jesus, and the disciples felt that Jesus had gone too far on this occasion. But Jesus justified His conduct by saying: 'Let them alone: they are blind guides. And if the blind guide the blind, both shall fall into the pit' (Matt. xv. 14). It is probably a proverb (cf. Romans ii. 19) and paints the Pharisees in an unforgettable picture. A peasant of Galilee once said to Rabbi Chasda[1]: 'When the Shepherd is angry with the sheep, he blinds their leaders.' It is well known that sheep will follow the leader blindly over the cliff to death.

The Pharisees are pictured by Jesus as blindly leading the blind into the pit. No sadder word can be spoken of those who pose as guides of light and truth. I once met two blind men in Cincinnati. One was a citizen there, and said that he was taking the other one around, to show him the city. It was more sad than humorous. On another occasion Jesus sadly said: 'For judgment came I into this world, that they that see may not see; and that they that see may become blind' (John ix. 39). This almost bitter word is recorded after the feast of tabernacles, only six months before the end, when the man born blind, healed by Jesus and cast out of the synagogue by the Pharisees, had his spiritual eyes opened also. 'Those of the Pharisees who were with him heard these things, and said unto him, 'Are we also blind?' (John ix. 40). They saw the point in the piercing words of Jesus, and understood that He meant to portray their spiritual blindness. There is a difference between having eyes and not using them, and having no eyes to use (Westcott *in loco*). The Pharisees were the shining example of wasted spiritual privilege. They had become blind by the non-use of their eyes. Jesus sorrowfully added: 'If ye were blind' (blind to start with, without responsible gifts of mind and heart), 'ye would have no sin, but now ye say, We see: your sin remaineth.' The Pharisees claimed to have superior spiritual perceptions, and could not claim immunity on the score of lack of eyes and minds.

The Pharisees asserted the right to dictate to Jesus how He should make good His claim to be the Messiah

[1] *Baba Kama*, fol. 52a. See Sanday and Headlam, Rom. ii. 19.

by giving them a sign from heaven (Matt. xvi. 1 ; Mark viii. 11). The answer of Jesus is partly ironical, but at bottom very sad, for 'he sighed deeply in his spirit' (Mark viii. 12). People usually profess wisdom about the weather in their section of the country. Some of the weather-wise gain respect because of the number of signs for the weather which they have. The one mentioned by Jesus is well-nigh universal and is a true sign, the difference between the redness of the sky in the evening and in the morning. Jesus finds no fault with this knowledge of the weather, but with the dullness of the Pharisees about the Messianic era. 'Ye know how to discern the face of the heaven; but ye cannot *discern* the signs of the times' (Matt. xvi. 3). The Pharisees failed as interpreters of religion and life. They were helpless to understand what went on before their very eyes because it did not correspond with their preconceptions. To-day the blight of mediævalism rests like mildew upon some ministers' minds, who cannot read the Word of God in the light of the present. On the other hand, some Modernists brush Jesus aside, as Himself out of touch with reality, and claim to have the vital spark of spiritual truth independent of Christ and the gospel message. It has always been difficult to read the signs of the times. The prophet sees beyond his age, and lashes his age into action to come up to his ideal of the future. His age slays him and the coming age builds him a monument. Jesus is here the prophet, and the Pharisees do not understand His dialect.

In Luke xi. 52-54 we have a dramatic picture of the conduct of the lawyers (νομικοί) who took up the cudgels in defence of the Pharisees : ' Master, in saying this thou reproachest us also ' (καὶ ἡμᾶς ὑβρίζεις, thou insultest even us), for the lawyers were the better instructed among the Pharisees (Plummer *in loco*). The last of the three woes for the lawyers (perfectly impartial as to number) is this : ' Woe unto you lawyers ! for ye took away the key of knowledge ; ye entered not in yourselves, and those that were entering in ye hindered.' This is a fearful indictment of the scribes, who were the interpreters of Scripture and of the way of salvation, but who themselves were on the outside of the house of spiritual knowledge, had lost the key to open it, and would not let others find it. The picture of Jesus drawn in the Talmud justifies this charge. Not simply are the scribes blind themselves, but they endeavour to keep others blind also. ' For ye lade men with burdens grievous to be borne, and ye yourselves touch not the burden with one of your fingers ' (Luke ii. 46). The lawyers had made the ceremonial and moral law far more burdensome than it was intended to be by their ' intolerably burdensome interpretations ' (Plummer). The record in the Talmud more than proves this indictment. Some modern lawyers are in the employ of men who pay the lawyers to show them how to evade the law. These lawyers were skilful both in addition of burdens for others, and in evasion for themselves. The best instructed of the Pharisees in Jewish legal lore show the utmost density of spiritual insight. So exasperated are this group of scribes and Pharisees, that outside the house they ' began to press upon him vehemently, and to provoke him to speak of many things ; laying wait for him (like a wild animal) to catch something out of his mouth ' (Luke xi. 54).

2. *Formalism* (Matt. v. 17–vi. 18 ; Luke ii. 37-54 ; xviii. 1-14)

One of the purposes of the Sermon on the Mount was precisely to show the difference between Christ's idea of righteousness, and that of the scribes and Pharisees, the religious teachers of the Jews. Many books have been written on this sermon, which has not always been understood. It is not a complete statement of all that Jesus preached, but it does set forth in clear outline the fundamental differences between Jesus and the rabbis. Jesus placed the emphasis on the inward reality ; the rabbis on the outward form. With Jesus spirit is the determining factor ; with the Pharisees it is the letter of the law, or rather their interpretation of the law, which is more binding than the law itself. Jesus puts God's kingdom before righteousness (Matt. vi. 33) ; the rabbis place righteousness before the kingdom. The Beatitudes depict the spiritual state of those who with a new heart are endeavouring to live the life of goodness with divine help and with inward joy. The 'woes' in Luke vi. 24-26 describe the self-satisfied Pharisees who love money and praise and power, the very opposite traits. Both Jesus and the rabbis appeal to the Old Testament, but Jesus seizes the moral content and intent, and lifts the ethical standard higher by going into the purposes of the heart, while the rabbis were busy with innuendoes and petty punctilios of the fringes of morality. Jesus reaffirms the moral force of the law and the prophets as interpreted by Him, but scouts the flimsy peccadillos of the Pharisees : 'For I say unto you, that except your righteousness shall exceed the righteousness of the scribes and the Pharisees, ye shall in no wise enter the kingdom of heaven' (Matt. v. 20). Did Jesus prove this daring arraignment ? He pointedly states that the Pharisees' standard of righteousness falls short of that required for the kingdom of heaven. He does not say that the rabbis taught no true things. This they did, as can be easily seen from the Pharisaic apocalypses and the Talmud and the Midrash. There are grains of wheat in this chaff in varying quantities. The best of the Jewish non-canonical books, The Testament of the Twelve Patriarchs, was neglected by the

Pharisees. If the Pharisaic conception of righteousness can be properly judged by the Talmud, the charge of Jesus is amply proven. Jesus gives the proof Himself in detail as reported by Matthew. I may say at once that I hold to the essential unity of this sermon. The proof given by Jesus applies both to the ideal and the life. Plummer is clearly correct in saying that Jesus is not referring to 'the hypocritical professions of the scribes and Pharisees; nor to their sophistical evasions of the Law.' He is challenging the inadequacy of the best that the Pharisees offered to men, even those who kept closest to the Old Testament itself. For even here they were content with scrupulous observances of the letter of the law. The six illustrations (Matt. v. 21-48) used by Jesus to show the superiority of His ideal over that of the Pharisees all get their point from the fact that Jesus is not satisfied with the mere external obedience to the Old Testament requirement about murder, adultery, divorce, oaths, retaliation, neighbours and enemies. Indeed, the ideal of Jesus on these points is considered too high and even impracticable by some modern reformers. Perhaps in the non-resistance argument Jesus has the Zealots in mind, and is opposing violence toward Rome; but even so one needs clear spiritual conceptions to be able to apply this loftiest of all ethical standards to avoid the absurdities of Tolstoi. The conscience of the world approves what Jesus said, but the world hesitates on the brink of the application, or, alas! flings it all to the wind in the mad whirl of war. But Jesus warned His hearers against the Pharisaic practice, as well as against their teaching about righteousness. Jesus is not ridiculing righteousness ($\delta\iota\kappa\alpha\iota\sigma\sigma\acute{\nu}\nu\eta$). Far from it. The rather He uses it as the synonym for the highest good (*summum bonum*) of the ancients.[1] The phrase 'do righteousness' is

[1] Cf. Stalker, *The Ethics of Jesus*.

common enough (Ps. cvi. 3 ; Isaiah lviii. 2) and is used by Jesus, in the sense of practical goodness (cf. the Epistle of James). But the Pharisees vitiate the whole matter, not merely by wrong teaching and evasive subtleties, but by doing righteous acts ' to be seen ' of men, to have glory of men. They not merely did these things to gain favour with God as *opera operata*, but to increase their reputation for piety with men. Jesus selects alms, prayer and fasting as typical instances of this hollow mockery and formalism. It is a bit curious that far back in Tobit xii. 8 we read : ' Prayer is good with fasting and alms and righteousness.' The Pharisees as a class have come to be mere formalists in religious life, as they were sticklers for the letter of the law. The picture here drawn by Jesus is in a way the most severe because it applies to the great mass of the scribes and Pharisees, and is drawn on a large canvas. The insinuation in John viii. 32, that the Pharisees are spiritual slaves and need to be set free by the truth that Jesus preaches, angers them very much. They are not merely the slaves of their own rules, but they are in the bondage of sin. Jesus insisted that even the Pharisees, the so-called righteous class, were the bondservants of sin. ' If therefore the Son shall make you free ye shall be free indeed ' (John viii. 36).

A long time after this Jesus bluntly said to the Pharisees who ' marvelled that he had not washed before dinner ' : ' Now do ye Pharisees cleanse the outside of the cup and of the platter ; but your inward part is full of extortion and wickedness ' (Luke xi. 39). It is well to have the outside of the cup clean. Certainly a cup dirty outside is not attractive. The language is difficult and is variously interpreted, but the most natural way is to take the second part of the sentence as the direct application of the figure of the cup or platter. The Pharisee cared much that Jesus had not bathed His hands before the breakfast, but he was unconcerned about the condition of his own heart. Proper form and etiquette are not to be despised, but the Pharisees 'pass over (παρέρχεσθε) judgment and the love of God.' The anxiety for scrubbing the pot clean on the outside has led to absolute neglect of the inside, where the food is which is eaten and which does the real harm. This food is full of deadly germs (extortion and wickedness). One result of this stickling for the formalities is the immediate vanity that insists on 'the chief seats in the synagogue, and the salutations in the market-places' (Luke xi. 43), a point in social etiquette which is strong in those anxious to have their place and prestige recognised.[1] At another breakfast with a Pharisee Jesus 'marked how they chose out the chief seats' (Luke xiv. 7). It was so noticeable that Jesus fixed (ἐπέχων) His attention on it, and spoke a parable about the embarrassment of such a custom. If three reclined on a couch, the worthiest had the centre, the next the left, and the third the right (Edersheim, *Life and Times*, vol. ii. pp. 207, 494). This emptiness of reality makes the Pharisees like 'the tombs which appear not, and the men that walk over them know it not.' Certainly this 'woe' is pronounced with the utmost sadness of heart on the part of Jesus.

At another time 'The Pharisees who were lovers of money' 'scoffed at' Jesus (ἐξεμυκτήριζον, turned the nose out at, Luke xvi. 14), because of the parable of the unjust steward. Jesus noticed the scoffing and said: 'Ye are they that justify yourselves in the sight of men; but God knoweth your heart: for that which is exalted among men is an abomination in the sight of God' (xvi. 15). This justification (δικαιοῦντες; cf. δικαιοσύνη) 'in the sight of men' (ἐνώπιον τῶν ἀνθρώπων) is what the Pharisees cared most about. In a word,

[1] Cf. Madame Esmond (Warrington) in Thackeray's *The Virginians*.

they prefer reputation to character. They had rather stand well in the eye of men than in the eye of God. But God knows (γινώσκει, as if by experience) the hearts of men, and reads beneath the formalism the facts of the case concerning the inner life. What is 'high' (ὑψηλόν) with men may be 'abomination' (βδέλυγμα) with God. We know that money counts more than morals with the average man. Even in business men act on the principle that might makes right. Politics is a realm from which preachers and pious people are often excluded. They do not know how to be practical politicians.

The formalism of the Pharisee is graphically presented in the immortal parable of the Pharisee and the publican engaged in prayer in the temple. The Pharisees 'trusted in themselves that they were righteous' (Luke xviii. 9). They were the standard of righteousness in theory and conduct, and even the judges of their own community. This complacency of some Pharisees is commented on in the Talmud, on the part of those 'who implore you to mention some more duties which they might perform.' So far as they are aware they have 'done' all the performances required by the Pharisaic rules. They stand ready to do more if they can be pointed out. This Pharisee 'stood and prayed thus with himself' (πρὸς ἑαυτόν) as Jesus almost facetiously pictures him. He addresses God, to be sure, but his gratitude is not concerning the goodness of God, but concerning his own superiority to 'the rest of men,' as, for instance, 'this publican.' He not simply had an exorbitant estimate of his own righteousness, but he 'set at naught' (ἐξουθενοῦντας τοὺς λοιπούς), treated the rest as nothing. The inevitable result of mere formalism is spiritual pride. The constant effort to reach the low standard of outward observance easily ministers to pride of performance. Hence vanity and conceit, constant demons in the path of preachers, beset the Pharisees with great success. They acquired an ecclesiastical pose, not to say tone, and expected to be greeted with due formality as 'rabbi' (Matt. xxiii. 18). And yet it must be said in defence of this rabbi that his claim to be moral was probably correct. Some of the rabbis described in the Talmud were men of unclean life. But, alas ! the Christian ministry is not able to throw stones on this subject, when the long centuries are counted. Thackeray in *The Virginians* dares to say : ' A hundred years ago the Abbé Parson, the clergyman who frequented the theatre, the tavern, the race course, the world of fashion, was no uncommon character in English society.' The Pharisees at any rate pretended to a holy life, and often attained it in externals. They had their spiritual fashions for phylacteries and for fringes on their garments (Matt. xxiii. 5), and were punctilious to appear at street corners, market-places, synagogues, feasts, and other public places 'to be seen of men.' They found joy in this constant appearance before the public eye. They had no daily papers or press agencies to keep them before the public, but they managed to be their own publicity bureau.

3. *Prejudice* (John v. 40 ; Matt. xi. 16-19 ; Luke vii. 29-35)

The charge of prejudice against Jesus is implied all through the long conflict with the Pharisees. They have prejudiced the case against Him. This attitude of the Pharisees has been specifically proven in the preceding chapter. Here it is only necessary to mention two or three words of Jesus on the subject. In John v. 39, Jesus commends the Pharisees for searching the Scriptures (ἐραυνᾶτε, indicative), but adds : 'and ye will not come to me, that ye may have life' (καὶ οὐ θέλετε ἐλθεῖν πρός με). They are not willing to obtain life at the hands of Jesus. He is to the Pharisees *persona non grata* and Jesus knows it. The will is set against Him and His message. It is a closed circuit. One may compare John vii. 17 : 'If any man willeth to do his will, he shall know of the teaching.' The Pharisees were prejudiced against both John the Baptist and Jesus. It is not absolutely certain that in Luke vii. 29-30 we have the commandment of Jesus rather than a parenthetical note of the Evangelist. Certainly it is very unusual to have such an interpolation right in the midst of the discourse of Jesus. We do have appended notes of the Evangelists added at the close of Christ's addresses. I agree therefore with Plummer, that here we have the contrast of the effect of John's preaching upon the people and upon the hierarchy, the contrast drawn by Jesus Himself. 'All the people when they heard, and the publicans, justified God, being baptized with the baptism of John.' They 'admitted the righteousness of God' (Plummer, ἐδικαίωσαν τὸν θεόν) in making this demand upon them, in treating them practically as heathen. The baptism was accepted in this spirit. 'But the Pharisees and the lawyers rejected for themselves the counsel of God, being not baptized of him.' They set aside as null and void so far as they were concerned (ἠθέτησαν εἰς ἑαυτούς), as not applying to them, since they were the recognised righteous class in the nation (οἱ δίκαιοι as opposed to οἱ ἁμαρτωλοί). Hence they refused baptism at John's hands, and were denounced by John for coming to his baptism in that spirit (Matt. iii. 7). As it was with John, so it is with Jesus, who now draws the parallel between the conduct of the Pharisees toward John and Himself. The point of the parallel is the bitter spirit of the Pharisees and lawyers (scribes) toward both John and Jesus, although these two preachers are so different in the very points of the criticism. The Pharisees found fault with John for being too abstemious

He fasted, it is true, but he was too abnormal about it, and did not conform to the regulated fast days of the Pharisees, though some of his disciples did (Mark ii. 18). Hence the Pharisees ascribed John's ascetic mode of life in the desert to the influence of a demon (M'Neile, on Matt. xi. 18). John was too peculiar for any use, and did not eat the ordinary food of the Pharisees. But Jesus was not a denizen of the desert. He moved in the common life of the people and ate their food. Therefore Jesus is 'a gluttonous man, and a winebibber, a friend of publicans and sinners' (Matt. xi. 19; Luke vii. 34). Jesus is thus too much like folks as John is too unlike them. So to-day the preacher is between the upper and the nether millstone of criticism. He is criticised if he does; he is criticised if he does not. The charge that Jesus was a friend of publicans and sinners is true, and Jesus took it as a compliment and justified His conduct in that regard, as we know. The point about being a winebibber and glutton is a gross exaggeration, and is mentioned by Jesus as showing the spirit of His enemies toward Him. 'They doubt whether John is a prophet, and they are convinced that Jesus is not the Messiah, because neither conforms to their preconceived ideas' (Plummer, on Matt. xi. 16-19). They are not willing for either John or Jesus to be himself and let his own individuality count for what it is worth. Rather they wish John to play at dancing, and Jesus to play at mourning at a funeral. Like sullen children in a game they pout when they cannot have their way with each detail of the game. Later the Pharisees will charge Jesus with having a demon (John vii. 20; viii. 48; x. 20). There is nothing quite so hard to overcome as this prejudice due to fixed preconceptions. As the Pharisees saw it, Jesus was weighed in the balances and found wanting. But Jesus rejoices in the fact that wisdom is justified by her works ($ἔργα$, Matt.) or by her children (τέκνα, Luke). After all, that is what matters, and Jesus shows His independence of Pharisaic criticism, and His determination to pursue His road to the end. He is not deaf to what they say, but He discounts it. They have become like common scolds, and it is impossible to conform to their whims and foibles, which vary with the days. The thing that does not change is their settled antipathy to any doctrine or rule of life that does not square in every petty detail with their own. It is possible for a modern church to fall into this Pharisaic groove in dealing with different pastors. Certainly the minister who sets out to please the world will find the world fickle as a flirt. The picture of the Pharisees as the elder brother (Luke xv. 25-32) who is angry at the reception given the returning prodigal is not a caricature. They not only limited the love and the grace of God to the Jews (or proselytes from the Gentiles), but to those among the Jews who followed the narrow path marked out for them by the rabbis in the oral law. This attitude amounts to a 'legalistic perversion of religion in Judaism' (Scott, Hastings' *D.C.G*). They were jealous and angry at Jesus for preaching to the poor and outcast. They are in a petty pout of prejudice because He does not confine His message to their social and religious castes.

4. *Traditionalism* (Matt. xv. 1-20; Mark vii. 1-23)

This criticism of the Pharisees by Jesus is involved in many of the incidents already discussed under the sections on spiritual blindness and formalism. But on one occasion this specific charge comes to the front in Christ's reply to the attack of the Pharisees for allowing the disciples to eat with unwashed hands. This attack was discussed in the preceding chapter, but the defence of Jesus takes the turn of a sharp counter attack, and it is just this phase of the matter with which we are here concerned. The Pharisees demand of Jesus: 'Why walk not thy disciples according to the tradition of the elders?' (Mark vii. 5). Thus the whole question of the Midrash or oral law is raised for discussion. Jesus does not evade it. On the contrary, He seems to welcome the opportunity to show how the scribes and Pharisees actually set their oral law above the written law of the Old Testament. This is precisely the position of the rabbis in the Talmud, as we have shown. The charge of Jesus therefore is not an exaggeration. 'Ye leave the commandment of God and hold fast the tradition of men' (Mark vii. 8). They are tenacious ($\kappa\rho\alpha\tau\epsilon\hat{\iota}\tau\epsilon$) of tradition and careless of God's word. Jesus accuses the rabbis of placing the *Halachah* above the *Torah*, as the Talmud plainly does. 'To be against the word of the scribes is more punishable than to be against the word of the Bible.'[1] 'The voice of the rabbi is as the voice of God.'[2] 'He who transgresses the word of the scribes throws away his life.'[3] Swete (on Mark vii. 8) doubts if the rabbis made this claim openly in Christ's time. We have no means of knowing how soon they put this contention into words. Clearly they were guilty of doing the thing in reality, for later it is an accepted doctrine with them. Matthew (xv. 6) reports Jesus as saying: 'And ye have made void the word of God because of your tradition.' Some of the MSS. read 'law' ($\nu\acute{o}\mu os$) here rather than 'word' ($\lambda\acute{o}\gamma os$), but the point is not material, since the antithesis is clearly between the oral teaching and the written law (Torah). The word for 'make void' ($\mathring{\eta}\kappa\upsilon\rho\acute{\omega}\sigma\alpha\tau\epsilon$) is the usual one for annulling a legal enactment. So we have it in Ps. cxviii. (cxix.) 126: 'They annulled thy

---

[1] *Sanh.*, xi. § 3.
[2] *Erubin*, fol. 21, col. 2.
[3] *Berachoth*, fol. iv. col. 2.

CONDEMNATION OF THE PHARISEES

law.' The Pharisees are charged with deliberate defiance of the law of God, because they prefer the traditions of men, as Isaiah [1] has well said (καλῶς, a beautiful illustration of what Isaiah prophesied). It is with the keenest irony that Jesus continues: 'Full well do ye reject the commandment of God that ye may keep your traditions' (Mark vii. 9). Swete (on Mark *in loco*) makes 'full well' (καλῶς) 'in part ironical.' To me it is wholly so here. Irony is a dangerous weapon, for the delicate edge is easily turned on a dull surface. Surely even the Pharisees on this occasion felt its keen point. At any rate the illustration of 'corban' used by Jesus makes it perfectly plain. This is a Marcan Aramaism.[2] Corban [3] = gift (δῶρον). It is a consecrated gift. 'The scribes held that the mere act of declaring any property to be *corban*, alienated it from the service of the person addressed (Swete, *in loco*). It is not perfectly clear whether, in the instance cited by Jesus, the son actually dedicated his property to God in haste, and was not allowed by the scribes to use it for the support of his needy parents, or whether he merely pretended to dedicate it while really keeping it for his own use (a more flagrant act, to be sure). But in either case, the point in the illustration is, that the Pharisees and scribes justified the son in his evasion of responsibility for the support of his parents, because he had taken advantage of one of the technicalities of the oral law. They cared more for the strict observance of their rules about 'corban' than they did about the support and welfare of the son's father and mother. So now the Pharisees had criticised the disciples for eating with unwashed hands. 'Rigid scrupulosity about things of little moment may be accompanied with utterly unscrupu-

---

[1] xxix. 13.
[2] Dalman, *Words of Jesus*, p. 139 n.
[3] קָרְבָּן

lous conduct in matters that are vital' (Plummer, Matt. *in loco*). This is merely one illustration. 'Many such like things ye do' (Mark vii. 13). The tautology [1] is effective. Jesus considered the matter so vital that He called the multitude to Him (Matt. xv. 10 ; Mark vii. 14), probably as the Pharisees withdrew in utter defeat and inability to reply to this exposure of the inherent defect in their teaching. Jesus makes an appeal for attention : 'Hear me all of you and understand' (Mark vii. 14). He announces what seems to us almost a platitude, so used have we become to the conception of Jesus, but to the Pharisees it was absolutely revolutionary. The startling statement is to the effect that defilement is what comes out of the heart, not what goes into the mouth. Jesus means, of course, moral and spiritual defilement, not sanitary rules of health. The Pharisees had made their ceremonial rules of diet a matter of spiritual life and death. The disciples themselves are astounded at this amazing and un-Jewish doctrine from the Master, and question Him about it privately in the house (Matt. xv. 12 ; Mark vii. 17). Jesus expresses amazement at their dullness of comprehension, and explains the parable in plain language (Matt. xv. 16-19). Peter was impressed by it, but it was not till after his experience on the housetop at Joppa (Acts x.) that he was able to see what Mark adds about what Jesus said : 'Making all meats clean' (Mark vii. 19). The power of tradition over men is tremendous in all ages. Jesus went up against the most immovable mass of it in human history. We use the terms 'schoolman' and 'medievalism' for the hair-splitting perversions of Christianity in the Middle Ages. But these men at least had glimpses of the spirit of Christ, a thing that cannot be said of the Pharisaic contention for tradition.

[1] Παρόμοια τοιαῦτα.

5. *Hypocrisy* (Matt. vi. 2-7; v. 15-23; Luke vi. 37-42; Matt. xv. 7-9; Mark vii. 6, 7; Matt. xvi. 5-12; Mark viii. 14-21; Luke xii. 1, 2; xiii. 15-17; Matt. xxiii. 13-39)

There is no dispute as to the hypocrisy of some of the Pharisees. We have already seen that six of the seven varieties of Pharisees portrayed in the Talmud by the rabbis are described as hypocrites. John the Baptist used the term 'offspring of vipers' (Matt. iii. 7; Luke iii. 7) afterwards employed by Jesus also (Matt. xii. 34). These severe terms may be subject to some qualifications. In the Talmud the six varieties are caricatures of the true Pharisees. In the Gospels the Pharisees as a class are arraigned as hypocrites, though we are not to understand that Jesus admits no exceptions. There were exceptions beyond a doubt, but we cannot soften down the words of Jesus to mean that only a few Pharisees were hypocrites, and that the great mass of Pharisees were acceptable to God. Jesus cannot be made to say that Pharisaism was the true exponent of the Old Testament or the adequate manifestation of the will of God for holy living. To be sure, the term hypocrite (ὑποκριτής) does not necessarily always carry the worst meaning of the word. Matthew is fondest of the word and has it fifteen times, while in Mark it occurs once, and in Luke four times. It was used originally of an interpreter of riddles or dreams, the reply of the oracle. The Attic usage applied the term to actors on the stage, who merely acted a part and recited the piece. It was but a step from this to one not on the stage, who pretended to be what he was not. The actors sometimes wore masks (cf. Mardi Gras to-day). Demosthenes (*Cor.* 321, 18) uses the verb for 'pretend' and Polybius (xxxv. 2) has the same sinister force. In the Septuagint text of Job we have it also (xxxiv. 30; xxxvi. 13). In Ps. of Sol. iv. 7, the Sadducees are accused of hypocrisy because of their Hellenising tendencies. It is open to us to say that the Pharisees who are designated hypocrites by Jesus were not always conscious that they were acting a part or were purposely pretending to be what they knew to be untrue about themselves. This distinction would inevitably exist. Jesus apparently applied the word to the Pharisees in both senses. In some instances it was all a hollow mockery, an empty shell; in others, the Pharisees are pointedly pictured as posing for the purpose of creating a false impression about themselves. This is the obvious implication of the words 'to be seen' ($\pi\rho\grave{o}s\ \tau\grave{o}\ \theta\epsilon a\theta\hat{\eta}\nu a\iota$, purpose, not result) the first time that we meet the charge in the Gospels (Matt. vi. 1, 2). The ostentatious piety of the Pharisees about giving alms, prayer, and fasting, is ridiculed by Jesus, with a touch of humour that bites like sarcasm. The picture of the Pharisee blowing a trumpet to attract attention to his gifts may be drawn from life or not. We do not know, though Cyril of Alexandria states that it was a Jewish custom to summon the poor by trumpet to receive alms, much as hogs on the farm are 'called' by the farmer to the trough, or children by the housewife. M'Neile (*in loco*) thinks that the trumpet was used in times of drought for public prayer and fasting. But the whole picture is comical in the extreme when we see the pious rabbi taking a stand at the street corner and praying with long and vain repetitions, so that the passers-by may see him praying. It is positively grotesque when we think of the disfigurement of the face [1] and the assumption of a sad countenance ($\sigma\kappa\upsilon\theta\rho\omega\pi o\iota$) 'that they may be seen of men to fast'

---

[1] King Jannai (*Sotah*, 22b) speaks of 'dyed' or 'coloured men, who pretend to be Pharisees.' One is reminded of the vanity of Herod the Great, who dyed his hair to show that he was still young.

(Matt. vi. 16). One is entitled to think that Jesus said these words with something of a twinkle in his own eyes, and that the people saw the palpable justice of the humour. To be sure, in a way many people were imposed upon by this procedure, and rated their rabbis high for their pretentious and punctilious piety. 'They have their reward' in full here (ἀπέχουσιν τὸν μισθόν).

In the papyri and ostraca this word (ἀποχή) is used of a receipt in full[1] for a debt. The Pharisees do get glory from men by the exercise of their hypocrisy, but they do not deceive God, who knows the motive in the gift, the prayer, the fasting. Hence Jesus urged secrecy in prayer. We need public gifts, public prayer, and public fasting at times, but these exercises easily become perfunctory and meaningless, and even evil in motive. Plummer (Matt. *in loco*) warns Christians against the easy peril of hypocrisy to-day when the papers and magazines give ready publicity to the gifts of church members, and easily stimulate false pride and love of praise. The Christian gets his recompense, but not necessarily in public. After all, the chief reward for being good is just goodness and the privilege of becoming better.

Jesus does not apply the term hypocrite to the 'evil eye' (πονηρὸς ὀφθαλμός) as opposed to the 'single eye' (ἁπλοῦς ὀφθαλμός). Here avarice is the Pharisaic vice that is condemned, but it is entirely possible that this *logion* has a backward look at the treasure laid up on earth (mammon), which is diligently watched with one eye, while the other is piously rolled up to God in heaven. 'Ye cannot serve God and mammon' (Matt. vi. 25), whether one is cross-eyed or cock-eyed. M'Neile separates these *logia*, but Jesus seems to blend them in Matthew's report. At any rate, Jesus does say 'thou hypocrite' to the captious critic who is quick to see the

[1] Deissmann, *Bible Studies*, p. 229; Wilcken, *Ostraka*, ii.

mote or splinter or speck (τὸ κάρφος) in the eye
of his brother while he has a long stick or beam
(δοκόν) in his own eye, of which he seems blissfully
unconscious (Matt. vii. 3-5; Luke vi. 41 f.). This
oriental hyperbole is meant to be a *reductio ad absurdum*
of the censorious spirit, whether in Pharisee or in others.
The Pharisees had acted toward Jesus in precisely this
spirit. The saying is probably a proverb which Jesus
has seized and used for his purpose. It is like our
'People in glass houses ought not to throw stones.'
Rabbi Tarphon is quoted as using this proverb to prove
that men of his day (about 100 A.D.) could not take
reproof. If one said: 'Cast the mote out of thine eye,'
the one addressed would answer: 'Cast the beam out
of thine eye' (*Erach.*, 16 b). But M'Neile (Matt. vii.
3) thinks that 'this was probably an attack on the
N. T. words.'

Toward the close of the Sermon on the Mount Jesus
warns His hearers against 'false prophets, which come
to you in sheep's clothing, but inwardly are ravenous
wolves' (Matt. vii. 15). These 'false prophets'
(ψευδοπροφῆται) 'can hardly refer to anything but
scribes and Pharisees' (Plummer *in loco*), though the
saying is true in a much wider application. False
Christian prophets did appear at a later time, false
teachers (2 Peter), even false apostles (2 Cor. xi. 13), and
false Christs. There had been false prophets in the
Old Testament times (Zech. xiii. 2). These hypocrites
look like sheep and pass as sheep till they turn and
rend the sheep, 'ravening wolves' (λύκοι ἅρπαγες)
as they really are. The use of wolf for the enemy
of the flock is common in the Old Testament (Ezek.
xxii. 27; Zeph. iii. 3). At a later time in the allegory
of the Good Shepherd (John x. 1-21), Jesus will
term the Pharisees thieves and robbers, because they
steal and kill and destroy and do not defend the sheep

against the wolves. The Pharisees winced under these words, and some of them said that He had a demon and was mad.

In the retort of Jesus against the charge of the Pharisees that the disciples had sinned because they ate with unwashed hands, Jesus branded the Pharisees as hypocrites at the very outset : ' Ye hypocrites ' (Matt. xv. 7) ; ' you the hypocrites ' (Mark vii. 6). Jesus proved the charge of hypocrisy in this instance by applying to the Pharisees the words of Isaiah xxix. 13 : ' This people honoureth me with their lips ; but their heart is far from me. But in vain do they worship me, teaching as *their* doctrines the precepts of men.' The tortuous use of corban, already explained, illustrated well the Pharisaic hypocrisy. The scribes and Pharisees were guilty of placing ablutions before love, technicalities before equity, the ceremonial before the moral, law before life.

When Jesus warned the disciples against ' the leaven of the Pharisees and Sadducees ' (Matt. xvi. 6), ' the leaven of the Pharisees and the leaven of Herod ' (Mark viii. 15), they exhibited a surprising obtuseness of intellectual apprehension. Accustomed as Jesus was to the dullness of these gifted men in spiritual matters because of their difficulty in shaking themselves free from the Pharisaic environment and outlook, he yet expressed repeated amazement that they could not perceive this elementary parabolic turn till he explained that He meant ' the teaching of the Pharisees and Sadducees ' (Matt. xvi. 12). On this occasion the disciples might have been confused by the inclusion of Sadducees and Herod with the Pharisees. For the first time Jesus warns the disciples against the Sadducees. Here a political atmosphere (M'Neile) seems apparent. But in truth the puzzle of the disciples was over the simple use of leaven and literal bread. They rose to no metaphor at all. At a much later time Luke (xii. 1) quotes Jesus as saying to the disciples : ' Beware of the leaven of the Pharisees, which is hypocrisy.' Perhaps Jesus did not mean to say that the leaven of the Pharisees, Sadducees, and Herod was precisely the same kind of leaven. At any rate in Luke xii. He proceeds to show how useless hypocrisy is, for everything that is covered up shall be uncovered and made known. ' Whatsoever ye have said in the darkness shall be heard in the light ' (Luke xii. 3). Hypocrisy is folly and is unmasked at last (Plummer).

One has little difficulty in sharing the indignation of Jesus against the ruler of the synagogue, who pretended to rebuke the people while in reality censuring Jesus for healing the poor old hunch-backed woman on the Sabbath day in the synagogue (Luke xiii. 10-17). Under profession of zeal for the law he showed his real animus against Jesus the Healer (Plummer). Jesus turns upon this contemptible ecclesiastical cad [1] who had rather keep his little rules than save the poor old woman, a daughter of Abraham, whom Satan had bound these eighteen years. The Master denounces all who shared the narrow view of the synagogue leader as ' ye hypocrites.' The rebuke was so effective that ' all his adversaries were put to shame ' ($καγῃσχύνοντο$), hung their heads down for very shame and could not say a word. They had at least a sense of shame left.

There are probably Christians who wish that Jesus had been more temperate in His language about the Pharisees, as He is reported in Matt. xxiii., or who even hope that the Evangelist has exaggerated, for dramatic reasons, the words of the meek and lowly Nazarene on this occasion. At least they will say that Jesus laboured under undue excitement and is not to be held to strict account for language uttered under such a nervous

[1] Cyril of Alexandria calls him $βασκανίας ἀνδράποδον$.

III.] CONDEMNATION OF THE PHARISEES   139

strain and in response to such severe criticism as He had undergone. We must face the facts of the case as they are. The extent of the discourse makes it impossible to say that we have only a momentary and unexpected outburst. We must seek a deeper justification for the violence and severity of this language if we accept it as a credible report of the words of Jesus. It is true that it is reported only by Matthew, but one suspects that it belonged to Q. At any rate, we have had already various terms used by Jesus about the Pharisees, quite on a par with those employed by Him here. It is rather the cumulative effect of the rolling thunder of Christ's wrath that makes one tremble, as if in the presence of a mighty storm of wind, thunder, and lightning. The storm has burst beyond a doubt. Let us first seek the reasons for its violence as seen in these seven woes upon the Pharisees. The psychology of this denunciation is simply the long strain of the attacks of the Pharisees upon Jesus, probably for three years, culminating in the series of assaults on this last Tuesday in the temple. Jesus had heretofore exposed the hypocrisy of the Pharisees, but after all His indignation was like a pent-up volcano that had to burst at last. The time had come for a full and final arraignment of the Pharisees, who far more than the Sadducees (with all due respect to Montefiore and others who have sought to push the odium upon the Sadducees) are responsible for the tragic culmination in Jerusalem. The Pharisees have hounded Jesus in Judea, Galilee, Perea, and now in Jerusalem. They are the wolves in sheep's clothing who must be exposed once for all. With the Gospel in one's hands, I do not see how it is possible to criticise Jesus for this fierce philippic against Pharisaism. It needed to be said.

We have various woes from Jesus already, as the four woes in connection with the four Beatitudes in

Luke vi. 20-6; the woes upon Bethsaida, Chorazin, and Capernaum (Matt. xi. 21-4); the three upon the Pharisees (Luke xi. 42-4), and the three likewise upon the lawyers (Luke xi. 46-52); and the woe upon the world because of occasions of stumbling (Matt. xviii. 7). M'Neile is by no means sure that these seven woes in Matt. xxiii. were spoken on this occasion. Allen notes that the sayings in Luke xi. ' are incorporated in Matt. xxiii., but without distinction of audience, in a different order, and in different language,' proof, he holds, of a different written source for Matthew and Luke. One may ask if Jesus never repeated His sayings ? Is it strange that He should describe Pharisees at different times and places in different language, but with the same substantial idea ? Plummer suggests that, since the author of Matthew is so fond of the number seven, he has here made an artificial grouping of the seven woes for dramatic effect, like the sevenfold woe in Isaiah v. Perhaps so, but one surely will not be considered uncritical if he holds that the discourse in Matt. xxiii. is too sedate and powerful for mere artificial compilation. Plummer admits : ' These seven woes are like thunder in their unanswerable severity, and like lightning in their unsparing exposure. They go direct to the mark, and they illuminate while they strike. And yet there is an undertone of sorrow, which makes itself heard when the storm is over.' The signs of life are here if anywhere in the Gospel of Matthew. The reporter may, to be sure, have balanced the various parts of the denunciation in literary fashion. Allen terms verses 13-32 ' seven illustrations of Pharisaic " saying " and " not doing," under the charge in verse 3 : " For they say and do not." ' M'Neile holds that the first three woes deal with the teaching of the scribes (14-22, verse 13 spurious), the second three treat the life of the Pharisees (23-28), while the seventh and last is directed

III.] CONDEMNATION OF THE PHARISEES 141

against the nation as a whole (29-33). With this Plummer agrees save that with him the seventh is transitional, treating somewhat both of the Pharisaic teaching and the Pharisaic character. One may note also that in the Sermon on the Mount Jesus arraigns the teaching of the scribes in ch. v. and the conduct of the Pharisees in chs. vi.-vii. We have seen what the Pharisaic outlook was on doctrine and life. Here in burning words Jesus lays bare the fatal defects in both.

Let us examine the charge of hypocrisy in each woe. The first woe is the most severe of all, for the scribes and Pharisees are the religious teachers of the people who look to them for light and leading. They are charged with keeping the people out of the kingdom of heaven who are trying to enter in (τοὺς εἰσερχομένους, conative participle). It is like sailors in a lifeboat who club away the drowning passengers in the sea who clamber up the sides of the boat. Only in this instance the scribes and Pharisees are not in the lifeboat, but drag down with them those who are trying to swim to shore. It is the travesty of ecclesiastical obscurantism. Luke (xi. 52) spoke of the key of knowledge that opened to the kingdom. Here it is the kingdom of heaven that is shut against men. 'A fragment of a Lost Gospel' (Grenfell and Hunt, lines 41-46) has it: 'the key of the kingdom they hid,' and the marginal reading in Luke xi. 52 is 'ye hid' (ἐκρύψατε). These so-called religious leaders 'hid' the key in order to keep the people in ignorance and death, the people who had shown a desire to find light and life in their enthusiasm for John the Baptist and for Jesus. The parallel is complete between this attitude and that of ecclesiastics in later ages who seek to keep the Bible away from the people in order to control the people by the priests. But other exponents of the kingdom are in peril of the same sin, when by their misinterpretations they hide the true meaning of the Scriptures from themselves and from the people.[1] It is obscurantism, not illumination. Their light is darkness. The saddest part of it all is that for most people the door that is thus closed is finally shut.

The second woe grows out of the first and carries it a step further, but draws a sharp distinction between the kingdom of heaven and Pharisaism. The Pharisees claimed a monopoly of the kingdom of heaven, but Jesus has already described them as outside with the doors shut by themselves. One must not confuse Pharisaism with Judaism. There were many proselytes to Judaism, but few to Pharisaism. The Gentiles would not be able to respond easily to the refinements of Pharisaism. But the zeal of the Pharisees was 'to make one proselyte' to Pharisaism, not to Judaism.[2] They had poor success at it, but when they did win a Gentile, the result was lamentable. The zeal of new converts was seen in the double ($\delta\iota\pi\lambda\acute{o}\tau\epsilon\rho o\nu$) emphasis of the new Pharisee on all the externalities of Pharisaism. 'The more perverted,' alas! Jesus uses very harsh language here, 'twofold more a son of hell than yourselves.' It is Gehenna ($\upsilon\grave{\iota}\grave{o}\nu$ $\gamma\epsilon\acute{\epsilon}\nu\nu\eta s$), not Hades. These preachers with their converts are pictured as heirs of hell, not of heaven.[3]

In the third woe (16-22) we miss the sonorous triplet, 'scribes and Pharisees, hypocrites.' M'Neile therefore argues for an independent group of sayings. The 'blind guides' ($\acute{o}\delta\eta\gamma o\grave{\iota}$ $\tau\upsilon\phi\lambda o\acute{\iota}$) reminds us of Matt. xv. 14. Plummer sees a more direct assault on the Pharisaic teaching, because of the specific charge of casuistry in the use of oaths (16-19), not legal oaths, but the use of common language in conversation. The

---

[1] Hort, *Judaistic Christianity*, p. 141.
[2] On the Jewish propaganda see Schuerer, div. ii. vol. ii. pp. 291 ff. Bousset, *Rel. Jüd.*, pp. 80-82.
[3] 'Sons of Gehinnom' is found in *Rosh. Hash.* 17b.

Talmud (*Kidd*, 71a) speaks of oaths 'by the temple' and (*Taanith*, 24a) 'by the temple service,' though this precise hair-splitting oath is not given. But it is of a piece with Pharisaism and is hardly mere caricature, to split a hair between the temple and the gold of the temple. In verses 20-22 the careless use of oaths is condemned. The temple is God's temple and God's throne is in heaven.

The fourth woe (xxiii. 23 f.) turns to Pharisaic scrupulosity in legal details of which the Talmud gives so many illustrations. The Pharisee had an abnormal sensitiveness about details in everyday life. These verses about legalism in daily (23-28) life correspond closely with the three woes to the Pharisees in Luke xi. 39-44. The law of tithing was scriptural and explicit. All 'the seed of the land' and 'the fruit of the tree' was subject to tithes (Lev. xxvii. 30; Deut. xiv. 22 f.), in particular the regular staple crops like wheat, wine, and oil. But the rabbis carried it to the minutest item. In the Talmud (*Maaser* i. 1) we read: 'Everything which is eatable, and is preserved, and has its nourishment from the soil, is liable to be tithed.' So also (*Maaser* iv. 5): 'Rabbi Eliezer said, Of dill must one tithe the seed, and the leaves, and the stalks.' These three herbs (mint, dill, cummin) were used for cooking, for flavouring, and for medicine. In Luke xi. 42 Jesus says that the Pharisees tithe 'every herb.' But Jesus does not complain at this scrupulosity with herbs. It was literalism, but not necessarily wrong. It is in the contrast that Jesus finds the hypocrisy. Coupled with this anxiety over legal niceties is a laxity about the weightier matters of the law ($\tau\grave{\alpha}$ $\beta\alpha\rho\acute{\upsilon}\tau\epsilon\rho\alpha$ $\tau o\hat{\upsilon}$ $\nu\acute{o}\mu o\upsilon$) like judgment ($\kappa\rho\acute{\iota}\sigma\iota s$, justice), mercy ($\check{\epsilon}\lambda\epsilon o s$), and faith ($\pi\acute{\iota}\sigma\tau\iota s$, fidelity), a noble triplet to offset the triplet of herbs. It is a common enough peril for lawyers, both civil and ecclesiastical, to cavil over technicalities. It is openly charged that American legal procedure more frequently goes astray here than the British, which cuts to the heart of the matter. Cases with us are sometimes remanded for another trial because the article ' the ' is omitted. The Pharisees thus have no monopoly in this travesty of justice. These blind guides are ridiculed by Jesus in an oriental hyperbole. Both insects and camels were unclean, and so forbidden as food (Lev. xi. 4, 42 f.). No one enjoys swallowing gnats either in his water or alone. It is perfectly proper to strain them out (διυλίζοντες, used of straining wine in Amos. vi. 6, 'through' or 'out,' not 'at,' a misprint in the A. V. for 'strain out' of Tyndale, Coverdale, Geneva), but the absurdity appears when these blind hypocrites are seen to gulp down (καταπίνοντες) the camel (hump and all)! To be sure, no one supposes that a Pharisee actually performed this culinary feat, voracious as some of them were. The whole point lies in the grotesqueness of the illustration. Camel is simply used for anything large, as in Matt. xix. 4, about the camel going through the eye of a needle. In the Klosterman-Gressman Commentary, it is suggested that we have a play on the word *gamlā* (camel) and *kamlā* for mosquito. But more to the point is the Talmudic saying (Jer. *Shabb*. 107) : ' He that killed a flea on the Sabbath is as guilty as if he killed a camel.' The camel was the most familiar large animal. Surely the people would be unable to restrain their laughter at this palpable hit at Pharisaic inconsistencies which were plain to everybody else.

The fifth woe (xxiii. 25, 26) is merely another form of the same rebuke, according to M'Neile, viz., that externals are valueless if important internal matters are neglected. But Plummer rightly sees a much more serious charge, since the tithing was legal, while the cleansing of the cups was mere tradition. This matter has been touched upon already, and need detain us only for a moment more. A certain amount of concern for clean cups and plates is certainly praiseworthy, but not if it is accompanied by heedlessness as to the way the contents of the cup and platter were obtained. ' But within they are full from extortion and excess.'[1] The meaning is that they use the immoral methods (Allen) of rapacity (ἁρπαγῆς) and greed (ἀκρασίας). This unrestrained desire for gain on the part of the ' pious ' Pharisees is strangely like the ruthless ' will to power ' at any cost, so the super-man has his way, attributed to Nietzsche, and curiously illustrated in modern business methods as well as in war. There is tainted food as well as tainted money, and tainted money can taint the food as effectually for the eye of God as the putrefying germs or ceremonial contaminations. It is an amazingly keen criticism of Pharisaic ritualistic legalism that is pertinent for modern men who seek to carry religion into business and politics, not to say war. Jesus advocates a thorough cleansing of the inside of the cup, in order that the outside may be clean also. No doubt such a wholesale washing would be of value in pulpit and pew to-day. But let us learn the lesson of Jesus, that the place to begin is on the inside. We shall care all the more about the outside, but the inside is what matters. This philosophy of life is revolutionary even to-day, with all our boasted progress and civilisation. The shell is still of more value than the kernel in many circles (social, political, commercial, religious). One may note in Edmund's *Buddhistic and Christian Gospels* (p. 84) : ' What use to thee is matted hair, O fool ? What use the goat-skin garment ? Within thee there is ravening ; the outside thou makest clean.'

[1] I should not press too much the use of ἐξ after νέμουσιν here in contrast with its absence in Luke xi. 39 as Plummer does. I rather think that the same idea is conveyed in Luke also.

The sixth woe (xxiii. 27, 28) is 'against external propriety which conceals internal wickedness' (M'Neile). In Luke xi. 44 the peril is from stepping on unseen graves, unconscious contamination. Here it is the whitewashed tombs with which the Pharisees are compared. On the fifteenth of the month Adar the Jews whitewashed the tombs in order that people might not touch them and be defiled (B. *Moed. Qat.* 1a). In either case there is defilement in the graves themselves (the decaying bodies), whether concealed or unconcealed. It is not clear whether in this charge Jesus means to say that the Pharisees are conscious or unconscious hypocrites. But Plummer notes that our use of the term whitewashing moral evil is more like the passage in Matthew than the one in Luke. The phrase 'whited sepulchre' ($\tau\acute{\alpha}\phi$os $\kappa\epsilon\kappa\text{o}\nu\iota\alpha\mu\acute{\epsilon}\nu$os) is one of those things that stick like a burr. It is much stronger than Paul's 'thou whited wall' ($\tau\text{o}\hat{\iota}\chi\epsilon$ $\kappa\epsilon\kappa\text{o}\nu\iota\alpha\mu\acute{\epsilon}\nu\epsilon$) applied to the high priest Ananias in Acts xxiii. 3. When Jesus spoke, the white-washing of the tombs was quite recent (done for the passover) and the illustration would be all the more pertinent.

The seventh and last woe (xxiii. 29-33) may be compared with Luke xi. 47. Montefiore (*in loco, Comm. on the Synoptic Gospels*) says that this woe is 'ironical, but also rather absurd.' But the absurdity lies rather in the inability of a cultured Jew to see the point of the hypocrisy of these Pharisees, who were at this very moment plotting with the Sadducees for the death of Jesus, the greatest of all Jewish prophets, while posing as superior to their fathers. They professed to be greatly distressed at the narrowness of their fathers who murdered the prophets. To atone for it they built beautiful monuments over their tombs. But by that very act 'you bear witness to the murder-taint in your blood' (Allen). These very Pharisees will soon shout, 'Crucify him,' when Pilate was seeking to

III.] CONDEMNATION OF THE PHARISEES 147

release Jesus (Mark xv. 13). It is true that the charge of building the tombs for the prophets slain by their fathers applied to the Jewish people as a nation (M'Neile), but the Pharisees were the religious teachers and instigators of moral ideals, and could justly be held responsible for this hypocrisy. The justice of the charge of Jesus is shown by the conduct of the Pharisees toward Stephen. He pointedly charged them with being betrayers and murderers of Jesus the Righteous One, of whose coming the prophets spoke who were slain by their fathers (Acts vii. 52). The proof is complete, for as Stephen spoke these very Pharisees who had clamoured for the blood of Jesus gnashed their teeth and stoned Stephen to death (ἐλιθοβόλουν, repeated action, Acts vii. 59). The murder-taint was in the blood of these men who put on airs of superiority to their fathers. There is no doubt of the irony of Jesus, but it is tremendously pertinent and in earnest. 'Fill ye up then the measure of your fathers' (πληρώσατε). One may compare John xiii. 27 : 'That thou doest, do quickly.' 'In spite of all your hypocritical professions, you are sure to prove yourselves worthy descendants of Prophet-slayers' (Plummer). 'Ye serpents, ye offspring of vipers, how shall ye escape the judgment of hell ? ' The words cut like a whip and stung like a serpent's bite. Jesus poured out a vial of 'the wrath of the Lamb.' There is a strange likeness to the curse in the Talmud on the house of Annas : 'Woe to the house of Annas ! Woe to their serpent-like hissings ! ' (cf. Edersheim, *Life and Times*, vol. i. p. 263). One draws the veil over this sad and terrible scene, but there is no need to apologise for Jesus. One is reminded of the words of Paul about the cutting off of the Jews and the grafting in of the Gentiles : 'Behold the goodness and the severity of God' (Rom. xi. 22). Listen also to the words in Heb. xii. 29: 'For our God is a consuming fire.' On this occasion Jesus spoke not merely as a man indignant over affectation, insincerity, and wrong in the guise of goodness, but as a prophet raging with a holy rhapsody of righteousness and jealousy for God, as the Son of God standing in mortal combat with the foes that had crossed His every path since He had left the devil defeated in the wilderness, these veritable angels of the devil, wearing the livery of heaven, and now engaged in the act of crucifying the Son of God under the pretext of defence of God's laws and God's righteousness. The very shock precipitated in this moment of destiny the acid of truth that has eaten its way through hypocrisy through all the ages. The hypocrites flinched and slunk away like maddened serpents before the blasting words of Jesus. But this immortal picture can never be destroyed, and no modern whitewash can cover up the rottenness of this hypocrisy. Jesus stands alone at the end of the controversy, but He has the eternal hatred of all hypocrites, and the undying love of all who love reality and hate sham.

6. *Blasphemy against the Holy Spirit* (Matt. xii. 31-3 ; Mark iii. 28-30 ; Luke xii. 10)

Luke gives this charge at a later time, but Matthew and Mark give it just before the first great group of parables. Matthew uses 'therefore' and connects the charge with that of the Pharisees. It is almost like the *tu quoque* argument. When the Pharisees accused Jesus of being in league with Beelzebub as the explanation of His miracles, Jesus retorts that they are guilty of blasphemy against the Holy Spirit. The Pharisees had already accused Jesus of blasphemy in claiming the right to forgive sins (Mark ii. 7). Later the Pharisees and Sadducees will condemn Jesus to death, on the charge of blasphemy, because of His Messianic claims

They will not have it that Jesus is the Son of God. The Pharisees place Jesus on the side of the devil. Jesus definitely accuses them of taking their stand with Satan against Him. It is easy to bandy words and charges, and after all the test of time reveals who is right. Jesus is waging war against Satan. Jesus appeals to the facts in the case. It stands to reason that Satan will not tear down his own work as Jesus is doing. The combination of the language in Matthew, Mark, and Luke raises some difficulty. Allen and M'Neile take 'Son of Man' as here a mistranslation for the Aramaic *barnasha*, man, and appeal to 'men' in Matt. and 'sons of men' in Mark as proof. It is possible, but by no means necessary in this context, since Mark has 'all' 'sins' and 'blasphemy' except blasphemy against the Holy Spirit. This will include blasphemy against Jesus in the 'all.' We cannot say therefore that the contrast is simply between blasphemy against men and the Holy Spirit. The passage as it stands admits that it was less heinous to blaspheme Jesus than the Holy Spirit. Jesus, though Divine, was also human, and His deity was approached from the human side. Men could repent of carelessness or failure about Jesus, bad as it was. M'Neile notes that in Jewish phraseology many sins were called unpardonable. He mentions deliberate sins (Numb. xv. 30 f.), the iniquity of Eli's house (1 Sam. iii. 14). There are also Rabbinic parallels like: 'There is no forgiveness for him forever' (Dalman, *Words of Jesus*, p. 147). But these instances do not detract from the solemn majesty of the doom pronounced on the Pharisees by Jesus. Mark puts it in the strongest possible form: 'But is guilty of an eternal sin' ($\text{ἔνοχός ἐστιν αἰωνίου ἁμαρτήματος}$). The act reaches into the next age and is final. But it is not the state of hardness usually expressed by 'sinning away one's day of grace' or saying:

'Evil, be thou my good.' It is very definitely explained as attributing the work of the Holy Spirit to the devil. Jesus specifically claimed that He cast out demons by the Spirit of God. He was engaged in the work of blessing men, and the Pharisees turned and branded His whole work as that of the devil. It is not possible to conceive of a more terrible sin than this. It is like high treason, the highest of all crimes against the State. This unpardonable sin is not necessarily a spoken word as here, but rests upon the resentment against God in the heart. Philo (*De Profugis* on Ex. xxi. 17) is quoted by M'Neile as saying : 'And what evil speaking could be more shameful than to say, not concerning us but concerning God, that He is the source of evil ? ' Dalman (*Words of Jesus*, pp. 148-154) doubts if Jesus used the words prohibiting forgiveness in this age or in that which is to come. This 'emphatic periphrasis' (Plummer) for 'never' is indeed eschatological, and is common in the apocalyptic literature of the first century A.D. (2 Ezra vii. 50 ; Apoc. Baruch xv. 7, 8) and in the Talmud (*Aboth* ii. 8 ; *Ber*. R. 44). This age and the coming age are often used side by side. Westcott (*Historic Faith*, pp. 150 f.) holds out the hope that in the end even those who commit the unpardonable sin will be summed up in Christ. Certainly there is no pleasure in contemplating the eternal damnation of any man. But the words ' eternal sin ' in Mark throws some light on this very dark subject. The state of heart that keeps on sinning seems to compel eternal punishment. No forgiveness before confession. Confession is in this case inconceivable. One has gone to the limit of a depraved heart who will deliberately attribute the manifest work of God's Spirit to the devil. To be sure, the natural meaning of 'eternal sin' here is an act of sin ($ἁμάρτημα$) with eternal consequences, but even so the point remains true that no one will commit this sin save as an irrevocable culmination. It is quite possible for men to come perilously near to this same sin to-day when the work of grace in the heart of man is by some ridiculed as a superstition and a delusion, if not worse.

7. *Rejection of God in Rejecting Jesus* (John v. 42 f.; vi. 52; Matt. xvii. 12; John vii. 48; viii. 21-52; x. 25-38)

Like a *Miserere* there runs a deep undertone of disappointment through the teaching of Jesus that He has to carry on His work with the active opposition of the religious leaders of the time. Votaw (*Biblical World*, Dec. 1915, p. 397) says that Jesus 'elevated Jewish ethics so distinctly, He reformed Judaism so thoroughly, that the scribes and Pharisees—the official moral and religious teachers of His nation—rejected Him; and the Gentiles of the Mediterranean world, whom Jewish ethics had failed to win, became converts to His gospel.' Jesus is conscious of the opposition all the time, and endeavours to open the eyes of these hopelessly blind leaders. But He consistently warns the Pharisees of their doom, and tries to make them understand that in rejecting Him they were also rejecting God the Father who sent Him. This point comes out more sharply in the Fourth Gospel, but it is present in the Synoptic Gospels also. Finally, the warning becomes doom, but the Pharisees turned a deaf ear, and thought that with the death of Jesus they had achieved final victory over the Messianic Pretender. The words of Jesus fall like those of a judge upon those who have wasted their opportunity.

The Pharisees have just made a formal effort to kill Jesus (John v. 18), when He explains why they will not come to Him that they may have life: 'But I know you

that ye have not the love of God in yourselves. I am
come in my Father's name, and ye receive me not; if
another shall come in his own name, him ye will receive'
(John v. 41-43). This irony was literally true, as the
case of Bar-Cochba proved. But note that here Jesus
accuses the Pharisees of being without love for God.
Jesus says expressly: 'I know you' by experience. 'I
have come to know you' (ἔγνωκα ὑμᾶς) to my sorrow.

When the Jews in the synagogue in Capernaum
'strove one with another' (ἐμάχοντο πρὸς ἀλλήλους,
John vi. 52) because Jesus claimed to be the bread of
life, better than the manna in the wilderness, He made
appropriation of His flesh and blood essential to life.
The Pharisees led the people away then and have led
them away since. Jesus early foresaw the miserable
outcome of the spiritual deadlock between Him and the
Pharisees. He predicted His death on the occasion
of His first visit to Jerusalem (John ii. 19). Toward the
close of His ministry He repeatedly predicted His death
(finally crucifixion) at the hands of the Sanhedrin ('the
elders and chief priests and scribes,' Matt. xvi. 21). He
saw clearly that, as they had done to John the Baptist
what they listed, so they will do to the Son of man
(Matt. xvii. 12). The vague connection of the Pharisees
with the death of John is noted in John iv. 1-4. The
rejection of both John and Jesus by the Pharisees
(Matt. xi. 16-19) would lead to the same result in both
cases.

Finally, Jesus defies the Pharisees openly as His
enemies at the last feast of tabernacles: 'Why seek
ye to kill me?' (John vii. 19). 'Where I am ye cannot
come' (vii. 34), he added. The Pharisees took this
condemnatory sentence as a confession of defeat on the
part of Jesus, and ridiculed His apparent decision to go
to the Dispersion, and give up His work in Palestine
(John vii. 35 f.). A few days later Jesus again said to the

Pharisees, that whither He went they could not come (John viii. 21). This time they sneered that He probably meant to commit suicide. But Jesus left no room for cavil in His reply: 'Ye are from beneath; I am from above,' and this: 'Ye shall die in your sins: for except ye shall believe that I am He, ye shall die in your sins.' These cutting words reveal the depth of the cleavage between Jesus and the Pharisees. They are on different sides of the chasm, with different origin, spirit, purpose, destiny. There is no 'he' after the 'I am' ($εἰμί$) in the Greek. Westcott (*in loco*) takes this absolute use of the verb to be a direct claim to be 'the invisible majesty of God; that I unite in virtue of My essential Being the seen and the unseen, the finite and the infinite.' If so, Jesus means to tell the Pharisees plainly that their rejection of Him involves the rejection of God. This is not a popular doctrine to-day with Jews, Unitarians, and others who take a lower view of the nature and mission of Jesus. But unacceptable as it may seem to many modern minds, I see no escape from it as the conception that Jesus Himself placed upon His person and mission as the Revealer of God to men. The Pharisees were quick to see the tremendous claim made by Jesus, and replied eagerly: 'Who art thou?' (viii. 25, $σὺ τίς εἶ$;), hoping to catch Him with a formal Messianic claim, in order to make a charge of blasphemy against Him. Jesus evaded their trap, but stood His ground. The talk grew more direct and personal between Jesus and the Pharisees. Finally Jesus flatly said that they were not the children of God, but children of the devil (John viii. 40-44). Of course, in one sense all men are children of God the Creator, and in another we are all born with the taint of sin in our natures and have to be born again into the family of God. But here Jesus seems to mean something worse if possible than an unregenerate state of heart, though that was undoubtedly true of these men. He accuses them of deliberately trying to murder Him, with doing the work of the devil for the devil, with utter inability to recognise the Son of God, and hence with being aliens to the family of God. They do not know either the Father or the Son, and hence do not belong to the family of God. The indictment is scathing in the extreme. Jesus is the test of love for God. He reveals God to men and also reveals men to themselves. We know whether we belong to the spiritual family by our attitude to Jesus the Son of God and the Elder Brother of the redeemed. So Jesus drives the wedge into the hearts of the Pharisees: 'Which of you convicteth me of sin ? If I say the truth, why do ye not believe me ? He that is of God heareth the words of God : for this cause ye hear them not, because ye are not of God' (viii. 46 f.). The only answer of the Pharisees was that Jesus was a Samaritan, and had a demon, and then in speechless rage they tried to kill him.

Three months later, at the feast of dedication, the Pharisees again flock around Jesus to get Him to say plainly if He is the Messiah, but Jesus answers : 'Ye believe not, because ye are not my sheep. My sheep hear my voice, and I know them, and they follow me' (John x. 26 f.). He insists that the Pharisees must believe His works, if not His words, 'that ye may know and understand that the Father is in me, and I in the Father' (John x. 38). The issue is always there, the irrepressible conflict. Jesus is the Revealer of the Father, and without Him they cannot understand the Father. A good while before Jesus had spoken that peculiarly Johannine saying preserved in Matt. xi. 27 and Luke x. 22 : 'Neither doth any one know the Father, save the Son, and he to whomsoever the Son willeth to reveal him.' Thus the key to knowledge of the Father is in the hands of the Son. On this point Q reinforces the Johannine type of teaching very strongly. After the raising of Lazarus John (xi. 47 f.) notes that 'the chief priests and the Pharisees gathered a council' concerning the problem of Jesus. The end was near at hand.

It was not merely to harry the Pharisees after their defeat in the great temple debate, that Jesus asked them the question : 'What think ye of the Christ ? Whose son is he ? ' (Matt. xxii. 41 f.). He argues with them in their *Halachah* method (Briggs, *Psalms*, i. liv.), but with no quibble. Apart from the current view that David was the author of Ps. cx. which the Pharisees accepted, Jesus shows the Messianic interpretation of the Psalm, which may have been new to them (M'Neile). But it shows clearly that the Pharisees are poor interpreters of Scripture, when they reject Jesus and wish to kill Him for claiming to be the Son of God as well as the Son of man. The mystery of the nature of Jesus remains, to be sure, but mystery is in everything at bottom as science shows. Jesus here uncovers the incapacity and insincerity of His enemies in their attitude toward Him. They are speechless.

Jesus made the Pharisees convict themselves concerning the justice of God in punishing them for their conduct toward Him. He caught them unawares by the story of the husbandman and the vineyard. When the husbandmen kept mistreating and killing the messengers sent by the householder, finally he sent to them his beloved son, whom they likewise killed. 'When therefore the lord of the vineyard shall come, what will he do unto those husbandmen ? They say unto him, He will miserably destroy those miserable men, and will let out the vineyard unto other husbandmen, who shall render unto him the fruits in their season ' (Matt. xxi. 40 f.). The Pharisees and Sadducees are the ones who answer thus. Jesus did not leave the application doubtful, but added : 'Therefore I say unto you, the kingdom of God shall be taken away from you, and shall be given to a nation bringing forth the fruits thereof' (Matt. xxi. 43). Then Jesus added these solemn words : 'And he that falleth on this stone shall be broken to pieces ; but on whomsoever it shall fall, it will scatter him as dust' (xxi. 44). Matthew further adds this conclusion : 'And when the chief priests and Pharisees heard his parable, they perceived that He spake of them.'

The case is made out and the verdict of Jesus has become history. The leaders in Jerusalem brought upon the city the doom that Jesus foresaw. The Pharisees with the Sadducees invoked the blood of Jesus upon their heads and upon their children (Matt. xxvii. 25). Pilate knew that for envy the chief priests had delivered Jesus up (Mark xv. 10). His wife's message about her dream aroused his superstition, and that intensified his sense of elemental Roman justice. Pilate had supreme contempt for the Jews, and in particular for the Pharisaic refinements as did Gallio in Corinth. But the public washing of Pilate's hands as if that could wash away 'the blood of this righteous man' is a childish performance and thoroughly Pharisaic in principle. The blood of Jesus is still on the hands of Judas, Caiaphas, Sadducees and Pharisees, and Pilate. The dramatic washing of the hands is a common enough symbol for freedom from guilt and suits the oriental atmosphere and Pilate's embarrassment.[1] So Lady Macbeth sought in vain to wash out 'the damned spot' from her hands. Both M'Neile and Plummer regard the disclaimer by Pilate as a later note added to the Gospel and as unhistorical. I confess that I fail to see

---

[1] Plummer quotes instances among the Jews (Deut. xxi. 6 ; Ps. xxvi. 6; lxxiii. 13; Josephus, *Ant.*, bk. iv. ch. viii. § 16), and among the Gentiles (Virg. *Aen.* ii. 719 ; Ovid, *Fasti*, ii. 45).

the cogency of this argument. Pilate was more noted for inconsistency than for consistency, and this nervous conduct is thoroughly in harmony with the rest of his behaviour about Jesus. The so-called Gospel of Peter says: 'But of the Jews no one washed his hands, nor yet Herod, nor even one of his judges (Sanhedrists), and since they did not choose to wash, Pilate stood up.' That puts Pilate in a more favourable light, too favourable, I think. But the sad fact remains, that the stain of the blood of Jesus does rest upon the Pharisees along with the rest.

Later the Sanhedrin will show the utmost sensitiveness about being charged with the death of Jesus: 'Ye have filled Jerusalem with your teaching, and intend to bring this man's blood upon us' (Acts v. 28). So the Sanhedrin said to Peter after their passion had cooled, and they faced the peril of a revived Christianity, if not also of a Risen and Triumphant Jesus. This apologetic attitude towards the death of Jesus is characteristic of modern Judaism, and at least reveals a kindlier spirit toward Jesus on the part of the modern successors of the Pharisees. Every Christian welcomes this new temper heartily, and does not wish to preserve a spirit of prejudice or of resentment. Certainly Christians should be free from prejudice toward modern Jews, and should not hold them responsible for the conduct of the Pharisees toward Jesus. We cannot build monuments to the Pharisees, but we can be kindly in word and deed toward those who still follow the rabbinic traditions. After all, Jesus was a Jew, the apostles were all Jews, Paul was a Jew. If modern Judaism is able to glory a bit in these great Jewish names, who will say them nay? If they wish to build monuments to these prophets whom their fathers rejected, we shall only rejoice, provided the monument is not erected on condition that we Christians disclaim the things for which they died. Let there be no mistake about that. We are not disposed to quibble unduly about metaphysical distinctions or to turn Pharisee ourselves in modern contention for tradition. But let us not forget that Jesus stands out in clear outline as the result of modern criticism as the one hope of the ages in whom both Jew and Gentile may unite, who alone has broken down the middle wall of partition between Jew and Gentile, and between both and God; but He has done this by the Cross, which is not to be set aside as antiquated, but to be lifted up as Jesus was lifted upon it. It is by the uplifting on the Cross that Jesus is able to draw all classes of men to Him. Modern Hellenisers still find the Cross foolishness and modern Pharisees still find the Cross a stumblingblock, but Paul, who was Pharisee and then Christian, found it the wisdom of God and the power of God. Montefiore (*Judaism and St. Paul*) finds it worth while to devote a whole book to Paul to prove how unable Paul was to understand current Pharisaism. But the effort is an anachronism. The best Pharisees of his day placed Paul forward as their champion and exponent against Jesus. If Paul knew anything, he knew Pharisaism. In many things Paul remained a Pharisee and boasted of it, though he flung behind him as worthless refuse the husks of Pharisaism when he found Jesus, the flying goal toward which he ever pressed. But the greatest of the young Pharisees of his day became the greatest Christian preacher of the ages. The man who knew Pharisaism best came to know Jesus best. He was able to relate the spiritual Pharisee or Israelite to Jesus. So then the breach between Pharisee and Christ is not unalterably fixed. The chasm can be crossed on the Cross, to which the Pharisees had Jesus nailed. It broke Paul's heart to see the Pharisees turn away from Jesus. He had to fight Pharisaism in the person

III.] CONDEMNATION OF THE PHARISEES 159

of the Judaisers within Christianity itself. But Paul loved his Jewish brethren too well to let their zeal for tradition cover up the gospel as they had the law with *Halachah* and *Haggadah*. Jesus resisted the Pharisees to the death to set the human spirit free indeed. Paul took up the same fight and urged the Galatians to stand fast in the liberty wherewith Christ had set them free. Freedom in Christ was purchased with a great price, the blood of Christ. 'He has given us new ideals. And He has given us something even above that. He has given us the power to realise these ideals' (Warfield, 'Jesus' Mission,' *Princeton Theol. Review*, Oct. 1915, p. 586). Let us preserve this ideal for progress and power. Jesus still prays for His enemies, for Pharisees of to-day as of old. Let us not make it hard for any who hear the voice of Jesus to come to Him. It was love that brought the cry from the heart of Jesus over the fate of Jerusalem: 'How often would I have gathered thy children together, even as a hen gathereth her chickens under her wings, and ye would not' (Matt. xxiii. 37). It was with utter sadness of heart that Paul said: 'But unto this day, whensoever Moses is read, a veil lieth upon their heart' (2 Cor. iii. 15). It is our task to lift that veil, if we may, so that modern Jews may recognise in Jesus the eternal Messiah of promise and hope.

LIST OF IMPORTANT WORKS

ABBOTT. *The Son of Man; or Contributions to the Study of the Thoughts of Jesus* (1910).
ABBOTT. *Light on the Gospel, from an Ancient Poet* (1912).
ABELSON. *Jewish Mysticism* (1913).
ABRAHAMS. *Rabbinic Aids to Exegesis* (Cambr. Bibl. Essays, 1909).
ABRAHAMS. *Studies in Pharisaism and the Gospels* (1917).
ALEXANDER. *The Ethics of St. Paul* (1910).
ALLEN. *Int. Crit. Comm. on Matthew* (1907).
ANGUS. *The Environment of Early Christianity* (1915).
ANONYMOUS. *As Others Saw Him* (1895).
ATZBERGER. *Die Christliche Eschatologie* (1890).
Babylonian Talmud (Rodkinson's Translation).
BÄCK. *Das Wesen des Judentums* (1905).
BACON. *Jesus the Son of God* (1911).
BALDENSPERGER. *Das Selbstbewusstsein Jesu.* 2 Aufl. (1892).
BALDENSPERGER. *Die Messianisch-apocalyptischen Hoffnungen des Judentums.* 3 Aufl. (1903).
BALL. *Ecclesiastical or Deutero-Canonical Books of the Old Testament* (1892).
BARTH. *Die Hauptprobleme des Lebens Jesu.* 3 Aufl. (1907).
BAUR. *Paul the Apostle* (1873-5).
BENNETT. *The Mishna as Illustrating the Gospel* (1912).
BENSLEY and JAMES. *Fourth Esdras* (1895).
BENTWICK. *Josephus* (1914).
BENTWICK. *Philo-Judœus of Alexandria* (1910).
BENSON. *The Virgin Birth of Our Lord and Saviour Jesus Christ* (1914).
BERGMAN. *Jüdische Apologetik im neutestamentlichen Zeitalter* (1908).
BERNFELD. *Das Talmud: seine Bedeutung und seine Geschichte.*
BERRYMAN. *Jüdische Apocalyptik im neutestamentlichen Zeitalter* (1908).

LIST OF IMPORTANT WORKS

BERTHELOT. *Die Stellung der Israeliten und der Juden zu den Fremden* (1896).
BERTHELOT. *Das religionsgeschichtliche Problem des spät. Judenthums* (1909).
BERTHELOT. *Das jüdische Religion von der Zeit Esras bis zum Zeitalter Christi* (1911).
BEVAN. *Jerusalem under the High Priests* (1904).
BISCHOFF. *Jesus und die Rabbinen* (1905).
BISSELL. *The Apocrypha of the Old Testament* (1890).
BÖHL. *Forschungen nach einer Volksbibel zur Zeit Jesu.*
BOUSSET. *Jesu Predigt im ihren Gegensatz zum Judentum* (1892).
BOUSSET. *Die jüdische Apocalyptik* (1903).
BOUSSET. *Die Religion des Judentums im neutestamentlichen Zeitalter.* 2 Aufl. (1906).
BOUSSET. *Jesus* (1906).
BOX. *The Ezra-Apocalypse* (1912).
BOX. (OESTERLEY and). *The Religion and Worship of the Synagogue* (1907).
BOX. 'Survey of Recent Literature Concerned with Judaism and its relation to Christian Origin and Early Development' (*Rev. of Theology and Philosophy*, August 1910).
BOX. 'The Jewish Environment of Early Christianity' (*The Expositor*, July 1916).
BRAUNSCHWEIGER. *Die Lehrer der Mischnah* (1890).
BREED. *Preparation of the World for Christ.* 2nd ed. (1893).
BREHIER. *Les idées philosophiques et religieuses de Philon d'Alexandrie* (1908).
BRIGGS. *The Ethical Teaching of Jesus* (1904).
BRIGGS. *Messianic Prophecy.*
BRIGGS. *The Messiah of the Gospels.*
BRIGGS. *The Incarnation of Our Lord* (1902).
BROADUS. *Commentary on Matthew* (1887).
BROADUS. *Jesus of Nazareth* (1899).
BRUCE. *The Training of the Twelve.*
BRUCE. *The Parabolic Teaching of Christ* (1892).
BRUCE. *The Humiliation of Christ* (1892).
BRÜCKNER. *Die Entstehung der paulinischen Christologie* (1903).
BUCHLER. *Das Synedrion-Jerusalem* (1902).

BUCHLER. *Das galiläische 'Am-ha-'Arets* (1906).
BURKITT. *The Earliest Sources for the Life of Jesus* (1910).
BURKITT. *Jewish and Christian Apocalypses* (1914).
BUTTWEISER. *Outline of the Neo-Hebraic Apocalyptic Literature* (1901).
CAMERON. *The Renascence of Jesus* (1915).
CASE. *The Historicity of Jesus* (1912).
CASE. *The Evolution of Early Christianity* (1914).
CHARLES. *Eschatology: A Critical History of the Doctrine of a Future Life in Israel, in Judaism, and in Christianity* (1899). 2nd ed. (1913).
CHARLES. *The Apocalypse of Baruch* (1896).
CHARLES. *The Assumption of Moses* (1897).
CHARLES. *The Ascension of Isaiah* (1900).
CHARLES. *The Book of Jubilees* (1902).
CHARLES. *The Testaments of the Twelve Patriarchs* (1908).
CHARLES. *Apocrypha and Pseudepigrapha of the Old Testament.* 2 vols. (1913).
CHARLES. *Religious Development between the Old and New Testaments* (1914).
CHEYNE. *Religious Life After the Exile.*
CHWOLSON. *Über die Frage, ob Jesus gelebt hat* (1910).
CHWOLSON. *Beiträge zur Entwickelungsgeschichte des Judentums* (1910).
CHWOLSON. *Das letzte Passomahl Christi und der Tag des Todes.*
CLARKE. W. N. *The Ideal of Jesus* (1911).
CLEMEN. *Primitive Christianity and its Non-Jewish Sources.*
COHEN. *Les Pharisiens.* 2 vols. (1877).
CONDER. *The Hebrew Tragedy* (1912).
CONRAD. *Die religiösen und sittlichen Anschauungen der alttestamentlichen und Pseudepigraphen* (1907).
COOK. *The Fathers of Jesus* (1886).
CORNHILL. *History of the People of Israel* (1898).
DALMAN. *Der leidende und sterbende Messias* (1888).
DALMAN. *The Words of Jesus* (1902).
DANBURY. *The Use of the Apocrypha in the Christian Church* (1900).
DANZIGER. *Jewish Forerunners of Jesus* (1904).

DAVIES. *The Relation of Judaism and Christianity* (1910).
DEANE. *The Book of Wisdom* (1881).
DEISSMANN. *Light from the Ancient East* (1910).
DEISSMANN. *St. Paul : A Study in Social and Religious History* (1911).
DELITZSCH. *Hillel and Jesus* (1867).
DELITZSCH. *Talmudische Studien*.
DENNEY. *Jesus and the Gospel* (1908).
DERENBOURG. *Histoire de la Palestine*.
DEWICK. *Primitive Christian Eschatology* (1912).
DOBSCHUTZ. *Christian Life in the Primitive Church* (1904).
DOBSCHUTZ. *The Eschatology of the Gospels* (1910).
DÖLLINGER. *The Gentile and the Jew.* 2 vols. New ed. (1906).
DRUCKER. *The Trial of Jesus from Jewish Sources* (1907).
DRUMMOND. *Philo-Judæus.* 2 vols. (1888).
DU BOSE. *The Gospel in the Gospels* (1906).
DURELL. *The Self-revelation of Our Lord* (1910).
DUSCHAK. *Die Moral der Evangelien und des Talmud* (1877).
EATON. 'Pharisees' in *Hastings' B. D.* (1900).
EDERSHEIM. *Sketches of Jewish Social Life* (1876).
EDERSHEIM. *History of the Jewish Nation* (1885).
EDERSHEIM. *The Witness of Israel to the Messiah*.
EDERSHEIM. *The Life and Times of Jesus the Messiah.* 2 vols. 3rd ed. (1886).
EDMUNDS. *Buddhistic and Christian Gospels.* 2 vols. (1902-9).
EERDMANS. 'Pharisees and Sadducees' (*The Expositor*, Oct. 1914).
ELBOGEN. *Die religionsanschauungen der Pharisäer* (1904).
ELBOGEN. *The Religious Views of the Pharisees* (translation).
Encyclopædia Biblica (various articles).
Encyclopædia Britannica (eleventh edition, various articles).
ESCHELBACHER. *Das Judentum und das Wesen des Christentums* (1905).
FAIRBAIRN. *The Place of Christ in Modern Theology* (1893).
FAIRBAIRN. *Studies in Religion and Theology* (1910).
FAIRWEATHER. *From the Exile to the Advent* (1905).
FAIRWEATHER. *The Background of the Gospels* (1909).
FARRAR. *The Life of Christ.* 2 vols. (1874).

FARRAR. *The Life of Lives* (1900).
FELTEN. *Neutestamentliche Zeitgeschichte.* 2 vols. (1910).
FIEBIG. *Talmud und Theologie* (1903).
FIEBIG. *Die Gleichnisse Jesu im Lichte der rabbin. Gleichnissen* (1912).
FORSYTH. 'The Conversion of the Good' (*The Contemporary Review*, June 1916).
FRIEDLÄNDER. *The Jewish Sources of the Sermon on the Mount* (1911).
FRIEDLÄNDER. *Die religiösen Bewegungen innerhalb des Judentums im Zeitalter Jesu* (1915).
FRIEDLÄNDER. *Synagoge und Kirche in ihren Anfängen* (1908).
FRIEDLÄNDER. *Rabbinic Philosophy and Ethics* (1912).
FRIEDLÄNDER. *Geschichte des jüdischen Apologetik als Vorgeschichte des Christentums* (1903).
FRIEDLÄNDER. *Zur Entstehungsgeschichte des Christentums* (1894).
FRIEDLÄNDER. *Das Judentum in der vorchristlichen Welt* (1897).
FULLKRUG. *Jesus and the Pharisees* (1904).
GARDNER, C. S. *The Ethics of Jesus and Social Progress* (1914).
GARVIE. *Studies in the Inner Life of Jesus* (1907).
GEIGER. *Sadducäer und Pharisäer* (1863).
GEIGER. *Das Judenthum und seine Geschichte.*
GEIKE. *The Life and Words of Christ.* 2 vols. (1879).
GLOVER. *Conflict of Religions in the Early Roman Empire* (1909).
GOGUEL. *Juifs et Romains dans l'histoire de la passion* (1911).
GOLDSCHMIDT. *Der babylonische Talmud* (1897).
GOODSPEED. *Israel's Messianic Hope in the Time of Jesus* (1900).
GRANT. *The Peasantry of Palestine* (1907).
GRÄTZ. *Geschichte der Juden.* 5 Aufl. (1906).
GREENHOUSE. *The Messiah and Jewish History* (1906).
GREENLEAF. *The Testimony of the Evangelists Examined by the Rules of Evidence Administered in the Courts of Justice* (1876).
GRESSMAN. *Der Ursprung der Israelitisch-jüdischen Eschatologie* (1905).
GUDEMANN. *Jüdische Apologetik* (1906).
GUNKEL. *Zum religionsgeschichtlichen Verständnis des N. T.* 2 Aufl. (1910).

LIST OF IMPORTANT WORKS

HALL. *The Historical Setting of the Early Gospel* (1912).
HAMBURGER. *Real-Encyclopädie für Bibel und Talmud* (1883).
HARNACK. *The Sayings of Jesus* (1907).
HARNACK. *The Mission and Expansion of Christianity in the First Three Centuries.* 2 vols. (1910).
HART. *The Hope of Catholic Judaism* (1910).
HATCH. *The Organisation of the Early Christian Churches* (1895).
HASTINGS. *Bible Dictionary, Encyclopædia of Religion and Ethics* (various articles), *Dictionary of Christ and the Gospels.*
HAUCK. *Realencyclopädie.* 3 Aufl. 22 vols.
HAUSRATH. *History of N. T. Times.* 4 vols. (1895).
HERFORD. *Pharisaism: Its Aim and Methods* (1912).
HERFORD. *Christianity in Talmud and Midrash* (1903).
HERSHON. *The Treasures of the Talmud.*
HERTZ. 'Jewish Mysticism' (*The Hibbert Journal,* July 1916).
HILGENFELD. *Die jüdische Apocalyptik im ihrer geschichtlichen Entwickelung* (1857).
HOENNECKE. *Das Judenchristentum in 1 und 2 Jahrhunderten* (1908).
HOLSCHER. *Sadduzäismus* (1906).
HOLTZMANN. *Die jüdische Schriftgelehrsamkeit zur Zeit Jesu* (1901).
HOLTZMANN. *Neutest. Zeitgeschichte.* 2 Aufl. (1906).
HOLTZMANN, O. *The Life of Jesus* (1904).
HORT. *Judaistic Christianity* (1898).
HOSMER. *The Story of the Jews* (1897).
HUGHES. *Ethics of Jewish Apocryphal Literature* (1910).
HUHN. *Die messianischen Weissagungen des Israelitisch-jüdischen Volkes* (1890).
HUNTER. *After the Exile.* 2 vols. (1890).
HUSBAND. *The Prosecution of Jesus* (1916).
ISAACS. *What is Judaism?* (1915).
JACKSON. *New Schaff-Herzog Encyclopædia of Religious Knowledge* (various articles).
JACKSON, G. *The Teachings of Jesus* (1903).
JACKSON, L. *The Eschatology of Jesus* (1913).
JACOBUS. *A Standard Bible Dictionary* (various articles).
JENSEN. *Moses, Jesus, Paulus* (1909).

JEREMIAS. *Babylonisches im Neuen Testament* (1905).
Jewish Encyclopædia (various articles).
Jewish Quarterly Review.
JORDAN. *Jesus und die modernen Jesusbilder* (1909).
JOSEPHUS (various editions).
JOST. *Geschichte des Judenthums und seine Secte.*
JUSTER. *Les Juifs dans l'empire romain.*
JUSTIN MARTYR. Gildersleeve's edition.
KAERST. *Geschichte des hellenistischen Zeitalters.* 2 vols. (1901-9).
KAUTSKY. *Der Ursprung des Christentums* (1908).
KAUTZSCH. *Die Apokryphen und Pseudepigraphen des A. T.* 2 vols. (1900).
KEIM. *The History of Jesus of Nazareth.* 6 vols. (1876-78).
KENT. *Makers and Teachers of Judaism* (1911).
KING. *The Ethics of Jesus* (1910).
KIRKPATRICK. *Through the Jews to God. A Challenge* (1916).
KOHLER. ' Pharisees ' (art. in *The Jewish Encyclopædia*).
KOHLER. *Grundriss einer systematischen Theologie des Judentums auf geschichtlicher Grundlage* (1910).
KRAUSS. *Leben Jesu nach jüdischen Quellen.*
KRAUSS. *Griechische und lateinische Lehnwörter in Talmud, Midrasch und Targum.* I. (1898), II. (1899).
KRÜGER. *Philo und Josephus als apologeten des Judentums* (1906).
KRÜGER. *Hellenismus und Judentum im neutestamentlichen Zeitalter* (1908).
LAGRANGE. *Le Messianisme chez les Juifs* (1908).
LAIBLE. *Jesus Christus im Talmud* (1900).
LAKE. *The Stewardship of Faith* (1915).
LATIMER. *Judea from Cyprus to Titus* (1899).
LEDRAIN. *Histoire d'Israel* (1892).
LEGGE. *Forerunners and Rivals of Christianity* (1916).
LEMAN. *Histoire complète de l'idée Messianique chez le peuple d'Israel* (1909).
LESZYNSKY. *Die Sadduzäer* (1912).
LEVIN. *Die Religionsdisputation des Rabbi Jechiel von Paris* (1869).
LIBERTY. *The Political Relations of Christ's Ministry* (1916).
LIGHTFOOT, J. *Horæ hebraicæ et talmudicæ* (1684).

LIST OF IMPORTANT WORKS

LIGHTLEY. *Les Scribes* (1905).
LUCIUS. *Der Essenismus* (1881).
MACKINTOSH. *Rabbi Jesus.*
MACKINTOSH. *The Doctrine of the Person of Jesus Christ* (1912).
MAHAFFY. *The Silver Age in the Greek World* (1905).
MATHEWS. *The History of the New Testament Times in Palestine.* 2nd ed. (1910).
MATHEWS. *The Messianic Hope in the New Testament* (1905).
MATHEWS. 'The Pharisees' (art. in *Standard B. D.*).
MATHEWS. *Social Teachings of Jesus* (1895).
M'NEILE. *Commentary on Matthew* (1915).
MEUSCHEN. *Novum Testamentum ex Talmude et antiquitatibus Hebræorum illustratum* (1736).
MIELZINER. *Introduction to the Talmud.* 2nd ed. (1903).
MOFFATT. *Theology of the Gospels* (1912).
MONTEFIORE. *The Wisdom of Solomon* (1887).
MONTEFIORE. *The Synoptic Gospels* (1909).
MONTEFIORE. *Aspects of Judaism* (1895).
MONTEFIORE. *The Religious Teaching of Jesus* (1910).
MONTEFIORE. *Judaism and St. Paul* (1915).
MONTEFIORE. 'The Perfection of Christianity' (*The Hibbert Journal,* July 1916).
MONTET. *Essai sur les origines des partis sadducéen et phariséen et leur histoire jusqu'à la naissance de Jésus-Christ* (1883).
MOORE, DUNLAP. 'Pharisees' (*Schaff-Herzog. Encyl.*).
MORISON. *The Jews under Roman Rule.* 4th ed. (1899).
MUIRHEAD. *The Eschatology of Jesus* (1904).
NASH. 'Pharisees' (art. in one vol. Hastings).
NABBAL. *Étude sur le parti phariséen* (1890).
NICOLAS. *Les doctrines religieuses des Juifs pendant les deux siècles antérieures à l'ère Chrétienne* (1860).
NORK. *Rabbinische Quellen und Parallelen zu neutest. Schriftstellen* (1839).
OESTERLEY. *The Doctrine of the Last Things* (1898).
OESTERLEY. *Ecclesiasticus* (1912).
OESTERLEY. *Doctrinal Teachings of the Apocrypha* (1914).
OESTERLEY. *The Books of the Apocrypha* (1914).

OESTERLEY. *The Evolution of the Messianic Idea* (1908).
OESTERLEY and BOX. *The Religion and Worship of the Synagogue* (1907).
ORELLI. *Old Testament Prophecy of the Consummation of God's Kingdom Traced in its Historical Development* (1889).
ORR. *International Standard Bible Encyclopœdia* (1915).
OTTLEY. *Short History of the Hebrews in the Roman Period* (1900).
PAULUS. *Les Juifs avant le Messie* (1905).
PETERS. *Wit and Wisdom of the Talmud* (1900).
PETERS. *Justice to the Jew* (1910).
PETRIE. *Personal Religion in Egypt before Christianity* (1909).
PFLEIDERER. *Primitive Christianity.* 3 vols. (1906-10).
PHILIPPSON. *Haben wirklich die Juden Jesum gekreuzigt ?* (1866).
PICK. *What is the Talmud ?* (1887).
PICK. *Jesus and the Talmud* (1913).
PICK. *The Cabala : Its Influence on Christianity and Judaism* (1913).
PICK. *The Apocryphal Life of Jesus* (1887).
PLUMMER. *Commentaries on Luke* (4th ed. 1909), and *Matthew* (1909).
POLANO. *Selections from the Talmud.*
PRESSENSÉ. *Jesus Christ : His Life, Times and Work* (1879).
RABBINOWICZ. *Kritische Uebersicht der Gesammt- und Einzelausgabe des Babylonischen Talmuds seit 1484.* 26 vols. (1880-6).
RADIN. *Jews among the Greeks and Romans* (1916).
RAGSPORT. *Tales and Maxims from the Talmud* (1910).
RAMSAY. *The Church in the Roman Empire* (1893).
RAPHALL. *The Mishna.*
RAPHALL. *Post-Biblical History of the Hebrews* (1886).
RENAN. *The Life of Jesus.* 23rd ed. (1896).
RIEGEL and JORDAN. *Simon, Son of man* (1917).
RIGGS. *History of the Jewish People in the Maccabean and Roman Periods* (1900).
ROBINSON. *The Evangelists and the Mishna* (1859).
RODKINSON. *English Translation of the Babylonian Talmud* (1898).
RODRIGUES. *Les origines du Sermon de la Montagne* (1868).

LIST OF IMPORTANT WORKS 169

Roi. *Neujüdische Stimmen über Jesum Christum* (1910).
RYLE and JAMES. *Psalms of the Pharisees* (1891).
SANDAY. *Christologies Ancient and Modern* (1910).
SANDAY. *The Life of Christ in Recent Research* (1907).
SCHECHTER. *Die Chasidim* (1904).
SCHECHTER. *Studies in Judaism* (1908).
SCHECHTER. *Some Aspects of Rabbinic Theology* (1909).
SCHLATTER. *Israels Geschichte vor Alexander dem Grossen bis Hadrian* (1901).
SCHMIDT. *Ecclesiasticus.*
SCHMITZ. *Die Opferanschauung des späteren Judentums und die Opferanschauung des Neuen Testaments* (1910).
SCHNEDERMANN. *Das Judentum und die Christliche verkündigung in den Evangelien* (1884).
SCHNEIDER. *Jesus als Philosoph.*
SCHODDE. *The Book of Jubilees.*
SCHÖNEFELD. *Über die Messianische Hoffnung von 200 vor Christo bis gegen 50 nach Christo* (1874).
SCHOETTGEN. *Horæ Hebraicæ et Talmudicæ* (1742).
SCHREIBER. *Die Principien des Judentums verglichen mit denen des Christentums* (1877).
SCHÜRER. *The Jewish People in the Time of Jesus Christ.* 5 vols. (1891).
SCHWAB. *Le Talmud de Jérusalem* (1871).
SCHWALM. *La vie privée du peuple juif à l'époque de Jésus-Christ* (1910).
SCHWEITZER. *The Quest of the Historical Jesus* (1910).
SCOTT. *Christianity and the Jew* (1916).
SEGAL. 'Pharisees and Sadducees' (*The Expositor*, February 1917).
SEITZ. *Christus Zeugnisse aus dem Altertum* (1896).
SIEFFERT. 'Pharisäer' (Herzog's *Real Encycl.* 2 Aufl. 1).
SINGER. *The Jewish Prayer Book.*
SINGER. *The Jewish Encyclopædia.*
SMITH, D. *In the Days of His Flesh.* 10th ed. (1915).
SMITH, GEORGE ADAM. *Historical Geography of the Holy Land.* 2 vols. 14th ed. (1908).
SMEND. *Die Weisheit des Jesus Sirach.* 2 vols. (1906).
SNELL. *The Value of the Apocrypha.*

SORLEY. *The Jewish Christians and Judaism* (1881).
SPARROW-SIMPSON. 'Liberal Judaism and the Christian Faith' (*Quart. Review*, Oct. 1915).
STALKER. *Trial and Death of Jesus Christ* (1894).
STALKER. *Christology of Jesus* (1901).
STALKER. *The Ethics of Jesus* (1909).
STANTON. *The Jewish and the Christian Messiah* (1880).
STAPFER. *Palestine in the Time of Christ* (1885).
STAPFER. *Les idées religieuses en Palestine à l'époque de Jésus-Christ* (1878).
STEVENSON. *Wisdom and the Jewish Apocryphal Writings* (1903).
STEVENSON. *The Judges of Jesus* (1909).
STILL. *The Jewish Christian Church* (1912).
STRACK. *Einleitung in den Talmud.* 4 Aufl. (1908).
STRACK. *Jesus, die Häretiker und die Christen nach den ältesten Aufgaben* (1910).
STRAUSS. *The Life of Christ Critically Examined.* 4th ed. (1898).
SURENHUSIUS. *Mishna.*
SWETE. *Introduction to the Old Testament in Greek.* Rev. ed. by OTTLEY (1912).
SWETE. *Commentary on Mark* (1902).
Talmud. Various editions.
TAUCHMA. *The Midrash.*
TAYLOR. *Sayings of the Jewish Fathers* (1887).
TERRY. *The Sybilline Oracles* (1889).
THEIN. *The Talmud.*
THOMSON. 'Pharisees' (art. in *Int. Stand. Bible Encycl.*).
THOMSON. *Books Which Have Influenced Our Lord.*
THORBURN. *Jesus the Christ: Historical or Mythical* (1912).
TOY. *Judaism and Christianity* (1890).
TRISTRAM. *Eastern Customs in Bible Lands.*
VAGANAY. *Le Problème eschat. dans le IV. Livre d'Esdras* (1907).
VEDDER. *The Gospel of Jesus and the Problems of Democracy* (1914).
VIOLET. *Die Ezra-Apocalypse.* Teil I. (1910).
VITEAU et MARTIN. *Les Psaumes de Salomon* (1910).
VOLKMAR. *Einleitung in den Apokryphen.*
VOLZ. *Jüdische Eschatologie von Daniel bis Akiba* (1903).

LIST OF IMPORTANT WORKS

VOTAW. 'The Sermon on the Mount' (vol. v. Hastings' *D. B.*).
WACE. *Apocrypha.* Two vols. (1888).
WADDY-MOSS. *From Malachi to Matthew* (1899).
WAHL. *Clavis librorum veteris testamenti apocryphorum philologica* (1853).
WALKER. *English Translation of the Apocrypha of the N. T.* (vol. viii., 'Ante-Nicene Fathers').
WEBER. *Die Lehre des Talmud* (1886).
WEBER. *Jüdische Theologie auf Grund des Talmud und verwandten Schriften* (1897).
WEINEL. *Jesus in the Nineteenth Century and After* (1914).
WEINSTOCK. *Jesus the Jew* (1902).
WEISS, B. *The Religion of the N. T.* (1904).
WEISS, B. *The Life of Christ.* 2nd ed. 3 vols. (1909).
WELLHAUSEN. *Die Pharisäer und Sadducäer* (1874).
WELLHAUSEN. *Israelitische und jüdische Geschichte* (1894).
WENDLAND. *Die hellenistische-römische Kultur in ihren Beziehung zu Judentum und Christentum.* 3 Aufl. (1912).
WENLEY. *Preparation for Christianity in the Ancient World* (1898).
WERNLE. *Beginnings of Christianity.* 2 vols. (1903-4).
WERNLE. *Sources of Our Knowledge of Jesus* (1907).
WESTCOTT. *Introduction to the Four Gospels* (1875).
WESTCOTT. *Commentary on John.* 2 vols. (1908).
WETTSTEIN. *Novum Testamentum Græce* (1751-2).
WICKS. *Doctrine of God in the Jewish Aprocryphal and Apocalyptical Literature* (1915).
WINSTANLEY. *Jesus and the Future* (1913).
WINTER and WÜNSCHE. *Die jüdische Literatur seit Abschluss des Canon.*
WISE. *History of the Hebrew Second Commonwealth* (1880).
WOODS. *The Hope of Israel* (1896).
WORSLEY. *The Apocalypse of Jesus* (1912).
WÜNSCHE. *Der Jerusalemische Talmud.*
WÜNSCHE. *Neue Beiträge zur Erläuterung der Evangelien aus Talmud und Midrash* (1878).
WÜNSCHE. *Bibliotheca Rabbinica.*
ZAHN. *Komm. on Matt.* (1905).
ZOECKLER. *Die Apokryphen.*

INDEX

I—SUBJECTS

AARON, 13.
Abbé Parson, 126.
Abraham, 20, 22, 26, 39, 70, 91, 138.
Achad, 32.
Adar, 146.
Aeneid, 156.
Alcimus, 13.
Alexander Jannæus, 13, 14, 25.
Allen, 140, 145, 146, 149.
American legal procedure, 144.
'Am-ha-'arets, 20, 22, 23, 44, 47, 76.
Amsterdam, 53.
Angus, 3.
Anna, 50.
Annas, 17, 67, 147.
Antigonus, 16.
Antiochus Epiphanes, 13, 21, 40, 48.
Antipater, 15, 16.
Antony, 16.
Aorist, 1.
Apocalypse, 48.
Apocalypse of Ezra, 10.
Apocalyptic literature, 150.
——— terminology used by Jesus, 112.
Apocalypticism, 112.
Apocalyptists, 43, 48, 49, 50, 111.
Apocrypha, 40.
Apostles were Jews, 157.
Arabs, 15.
Aramaic, 149.
Archelaus, 21, 98.
Aretas, 15.
Aristobulus, 14, 15, 17.

Armenia, 15.
Assidean, 13, 17.
Assumption of Moses, 99.
Astrology, 33.
Astronomy, 33.
Athronges, 98.
Attitude of Talmud towards Jesus 51 ff.
Avarice, 135.

BABYLONIA, 11.
Babylonian Gemara, 34.
——— Jews, 52.
Babylonian Talmud, 11, 24, 34.
Bacher, 32.
Baldensperger, 42.
Balmforth, 61.
Barabbas, 99.
Bar-Cochba, 41, 57, 99, 107, 152.
Beatitudes, 139.
Beelzebub, 84, 148.
Bengel, 115.
Ben Pandira, 54.
Ben Stada, 54.
Bethsaida, 62, 140.
Bible, 139, 141.
Big Endians, 27.
Bitterness between Jews and Christians, 53.
Blame for Christ's death, 28.
Blasphemy against the Holy Spirit, 148.
Book of Jubilees, 43, 45.
Bousset, 3, 142.
Box, 7, 28.
Brahmanism, 25.

INDEX

Briggs, 155.
Broadus, 87.
Brutus, 16.
Buchler, 27, 94.
Buddhist, 7, 9.
Burket, 41, 49.

CÆSAR, 15, 16, 94, 107, 108.
Caiaphas, 17, 56, 75, 92, 156.
Calvinists, 37.
Camel, 144.
Cameronians, 20.
Capernaum, 53, 71, 113, 140, 152.
Caricatures of true Pharisees, 133.
Case, 3, 12.
Cassius, 16.
Caste system of India, 22.
Celsus, 58.
Ceremonial ritualism, 114, 132.
Chandler, 103.
Chapman, 103.
Charles, 9, 43, 48, 49.
Children of God, 152.
Chorazin, 62, 140.
Christ and the Hillel School, 28.
Christians, 53, 57, 79, 135, 157.
Christianity, 53, 61, 82, 104, 110, 132, 157.
Christian Church, 49.
—— Scientist, 7.
Chwolson, 28.
Condor, 108.
Confucianism, 9.
Confucius, 52.
Conybeare, 3.
Cook, 49.
Corban, 96, 131, 137.
Corinth, 105, 156.
Cornelius, 47.
Coverdale, 144.
Cyril of Alexandria, 134, 138.

DALMAN, 42, 53, 54, 131, 149, 150.
Daniel, 48.
Danziger, 49.
David, 88, 155.

Defence of Parables, 116.
Deissmann, 135.
Demonology, 84.
Demosthenes, 133.
Destruction of Jerusalem, 10, 22, 61.
Deutsch, 51.
Dewick, 49.
Diogenes Laertius, 52.
Disciples of John, 70, 82.
Dispersion, 152.
Divine sovereignty, 37.
Dobschütz, 49.
Drews, 3.

ECCLESIASTICS, 67.
Edersheim, 33, 42, 72, 77, 80, 97, 124, 147.
Edmunds, 145.
Eisegesis, 30.
Elbogen, 28, 36.
Eleazer, 12, 13.
Eli, 149.
Elijah, 92.
Elizabeth, 50.
English Puritans, 20.
Enoch, 41, 42, 48.
Epistle of Aristeas, 52.
Epistles of Paul, 9, 60.
Essenes, 5, 12, 22, 37.
Etiquette at a feast, 97.
Europe, 88.
Evangelist, 138.
Exegesis, 30.
Ezekiel, 48.
Ezra, 18.
—— the scribe, 28.

FALSE CHRISTS, 136.
False Christian prophets, 136.
False witness, 102 ff.
Farrar, 26, 31, 32, 52.
Fate, 37.
Feast of Dedication, 73, 154.
—— of Levi, 81, 82, 113.
—— of Tabernacles, 97, 118, 152.

Features of Pharisaic Theology:
(1) Divine sovereignty, 37.
(2) Oral law on par with Old Testament, 38.
(3) Belief in future life, 39.
(4) Messianic expectations, 40.
First Passover, 68.
Formalism, 120 ff.
Freedom in Christ, 159.

GALATIANS, 159.
Galilean ministry, 83.
Galilee, 71, 73, 79, 86, 87, 92.
Gallio, 105, 156.
Gamaliel, 21, 35, 64, 98, 100.
Gehenna, 87, 142.
Geneva, 144.
Gennesaret, 93.
Gentile, 11, 23, 29, 43, 46, 47, 60, 77, 78, 129, 142, 147, 151.
German critics, 85.
Golden Rule, 35, 52.
Good Shepherd, 64, 85, 136.
Gospels, 9, 51, 54, 55, 60, 61, 62, 63, 65, 106.
Gospel of Peter, 157.
Gould, 67.
Graft, 67.
Greek contempt for the body, 40.
Greenleaf, 103.
Grenfell and Hunt, 141.
Grounds of Pharisaic dislike of Jesus:
(1) Assumption of Messianic authority, 66.
(2) Downright blasphemy, 71.
(3) Intolerable association with publicans and sinners, 76.
(4) Irreligious neglect of fasting, 81.
(5) The Devil Incarnate, 83.
(6) A regular Sabbath-breaker, 85.
(7) Utterly inadequate signs, 90.
(8) Insolent defiance of tradition, 93.
(9) An ignorant impostor, 97.
(10) Plotting to destroy the temple, 102.
(11) High treason against Cæsar, 104.
Gulliver's Travels, 27.

HADES, 142.
Hadrian, 41, 99.
Haggadah, 30, 32, 33, 34, 36, 44, 95, 159.
Hagiographa, 28.
Halachah, 30, 31, 32, 33, 34, 36, 44, 95, 130, 155, 159.
Hanan, 67.
Harnack, 41, 62, 65.
Hatred of Jesus shown in the Talmud, 56.
Headlam, 118.
Heart of criticism of Jesus, 2.
Heart of the subject, 65.
Heitmüller, 99.
Hellenisers, 17, 37.
Herford, 5, 6, 7, 8, 10, 11, 18, 23, 29, 30, 31, 32, 33, 36, 43, 44, 51, 53, 54, 55, 70, 71, 101, 104, 113.
Herod Antipas, 64, 69, 137, 138, 157.
Herodians, 20, 21, 69, 89, 91, 106, 115.
Herod the Great, 16, 102.
Hillel, 18, 27, 35, 52, 65, 95.
Historicity of Jesus, 3, 4.
Holy Spirit, 148, 149, 150.
Hosea, 88.
Hort, 95, 142.
Hughes, 49, 63, 99.
Human free agency, 37.
Husbandman and vineyard, 155.
Hypocrite—the word, 133.
Hyrcanus, John, 12, 13, 14. 43.

ILLEGALITIES IN THE TRIAL OF JESUS, 103.
Inadequate signs, 90.

INDEX

Innes, 103.
Insects, 144.
Interpolation, 127.
Isaiah, 116, 117, 131.
Isocrates, 52.
Isaac, 39.

JACOB, 39.
Jason, 17.
Jehovah, 32.
Jesus:
  Accused of departing from the moral standard of the Old Testament, 78.
  Accused of practising magic, 55.
  Associated with the masses, 76.
  Assumes the prerogative of God, 71, 74.
  Authority challenged, 68, 94, 102.
  Bastard, called, 55, 101.
  Bore witness of Himself, 100.
  Bread of Life, 152.
  Breakfasts with Pharisees, 96, 124.
  Called a fool, 54.
  Called a liar, 55.
  Cause of rejection, 8, 43.
  Cleansed the temple, 67.
  Commends the general tenor of Pharisaic instruction, 1.
  Condemned Pharisaism, 43.
  Conduct on the Sabbath, 86.
  Deceiver, 55.
  Defies Pharisees, 72.
  Dines with Pharisee, 90.
  Eternal Messiah, 159.
  Fasting, 82.
  Forgave sins, 71.
  Gave sign of His Resurrection, 102.
  God His father, 73.
  God the source of His teaching, 100.
  Grieves over Pharisees, 115.
  Harmless enthusiast, 107.
  Hatred, 54.
  Healer, 138.
  Heals on the Sabbath, 72, 86, 89, 90, 138.
  Hostility toward Him, 66.
  Human, 149.
  Interpreter of Pharisaism, 5.
  Jew, 157.
  Jewish view, 58.
  Jews begin to persecute, 86.
  Josephus' description, 40.
  Judge of the Sanhedrin, 92.
  Lack of Pharisaic training, 100.
  Leader of Rabbinic School, 94.
  Likened to Balaam, 55.
  Messiah, 41.
  Messianic claim, 67, 68.
  Miracles, 91.
  Mystery of His nature, 155.
  Name in the Talmud, 53.
  Nazarene, 55.
  On the defensive, 67.
  Paranoiac, 85.
  Pharisaic instinct toward, 71.
  —— opposition, 69.
  Picture in the Talmud, 120.
  Political accusation before Pilate, 105.
  Popular idol, 98.
  Power to forgive sins, 71.
  Prays for His enemies, 159.
  Predicts death, 152.
  Reformed Judaism, 151.
  Refuted Sadducees, 39.
  Regulated fast days, 128.
  Revealer of God, 113, 153.
  Samaritan, 84, 154.
  Secret of apparent success, 98.
  Sign of Resurrection, 102.
  Son of David, 74.
  —— of God, 75, 107, 148, 149, 155.
  —— of Man, 73, 149.
  Test of love for God, 154.
  Three accusations, 105.

Jesus—*continued*—
  Used words similar to words of Josephus, 39.
  Warns against conduct of the Pharisees, 2.
  —— against the Sadducees, 137.
  Woes pronounced, 61.
  Wrath, 139.
Jewish Christian, 61.
—— Fathers, 38.
—— hate wins, 108.
—— hatred shown in early Christian writings, 56.
—— Prayer Book, 47.
—— Synod at Petrikau, 53.
—— Temple, 41.
John, 21, 50, 58, 65, 106.
—— the Baptist, 49, 50, 62, 63, 65, 66, 69, 70, 71, 81, 82, 92, 99, 127, 128, 133, 141, 152.
Jonah, 91.
Joppa, 44, 132.
Joseph, 50.
—— of Arimathea, 64, 76.
Josephus, 4, 5, 9, 10, 11, 12, 13, 14, 30, 36, 37, 38, 39, 40, 41, 44, 46, 47, 48, 87, 98, 99, 156.
Joshua, 30.
Judaisers, 159.
Judaism, 2, 5, 11, 18, 21, 22, 23, 29, 43, 50, 53, 59, 67, 82, 104, 129.
Judas, 156.
Judas of Galilee, 98.
Julius Cæsar, 15, 16.
Justin Martyr, 56, 57, 101.

KENNEDY, 49.
Kingdom of God, 58, 64, 111.
King Jannai, 134.
Klosterman - Gressman *Commentary*, 144.
Kohler, 2, 4, 6, 9, 19.
Koine, 116.

LADY MACBETH, 156.
Laible, 53, 54, 55.

Lake, 111, 112, 114.
Lakish, 18.
Law, Hastings' *D. B.*, 96.
Law from Sinai, 30.
Lawyer(s), 94, 119, 120, 143.
Lazarus, 91, 104, 155.
Learning the Oral Law, 38 f.
Leaven of the Pharisees and Sadducees, 137.
Legend of the Wandering Jew, 108.
Leszynsky, 20.
Levi, 77, 78, 80, 81, 82.
Levin, 53.
Levites, 63.
Levitical laws, 46.
—— purification, 27.
Lightfoot, 87.
Liliputians, 27.
Little Endians, 27.
Logia, 62.
Luke, 61, 80, 85, 89, 116.
Lydda, 56.

MACCABEAN DYNASTY, 10, 13.
Maccabeus, Jonathan, 12, 17.
—— Judas, 12, 17.
—— Simon, 17.
Machaerus, 69.
M'Neile, 73, 74, 75, 76, 77, 83, 93, 94, 95, 96, 128, 134, 135, 136, 137, 140, 142, 144, 146, 147, 149, 150, 155, 156.
Magic, 33.
Manana, 24.
Marcan Aramaism, 131.
Mardi Gras, 133.
Margoliouth, 94.
Mark, 62, 116.
Mary, 50, 54, 55, 56.
Mattathias, 17, 46.
Matthew, 65.
Matthews, Shailer, 9.
Medicine, 33.
Menelaus, 17.
Messiah, 40, 66, 85, 92.

INDEX

Messianic Expectations, 4, 12, 42, 43, 148.
—— Pretender, 151.
Micah, 117.
Middle Ages, 132.
Mielziner, 29.
Miserere, 151.
Mithridates, 15.
Moderate Jewish writers, 6.
Modern Criticism, 8, 62, 158.
—— Jews, 7, 153, 159.
—— Judaism, 2, 52, 157.
—— Hellenisers, 158.
—— Pharisees, 158.
Modernists, 119.
Moffatt, 65.
Mohammedan, 7.
Monotheism, 36.
Montefiore, 5, 6, 7, 8, 11, 53, 59, 60, 61, 62, 95, 102, 103, 139, 146, 158.
Moore, 52.
Mormen, 7.
Moses, 30, 31, 46, 103, 117.
Mysticism, 33.

NEW TESTAMENT WRITERS, 11.
Nicodemus, 27, 64, 67, 68, 76, 111, 112, 113, 115.
Nietzsche, 145.

OATHS, 143.
Obscurantism, 142.
Octavius, 16.
Oesterley, 4, 7, 28, 34, 72, 81.
Offspring of vipers, 66, 147.
Oral Law, 30, 33, 68, 96, 130.
Origen, 54, 58.
Origin of the charge of Blasphemy, 73.
—— of Christianity, 3.
Ostraca, 135.
Ovid, 156.

PALESTINE, 11.
Palestinian Judaism, 2, 3.

Palestinian (Jerusalem) Talmud, 11.
Pandira, 58.
Papyri, 135.
Parthians, 16.
Passion Week, 68.
Paul, 5, 6, 18, 21, 33, 35, 43, 51, 59, 60, 82, 105, 147, 157, 158.
Pentateuch, 28, 30, 39.
Perea, 74, 80, 92.
Perean Ministry, 85.
Personal God, 37.
Peter, 21, 44, 47, 58, 59, 65, 76, 115, 132, 157.
Pharisaic Apocalypses, 121.
—— Christians, 78.
—— Inspectors, 71.
—— Mystics, 49.
—— outlook on doctrine and life, 1.
—— Puritanism, 76.
—— Theology, 84, 91, 113.
Pharisaism :
   Apologist of, 33. 51.
   Emptiness revealed, 101.
   Few proselytes, 142.
   Husks of, 158.
   Inside view, 10.
   Misunderstood, 6.
   Paul the pride of, 5.
   Peril of, 110.
   Perversion of, 24.
   Philippic against, 139.
   Real Judaism, 60.
   Religion of official Judaism, 22.
   Roots of, 18.
   Schools, 27.
   Source, 27.
   Source of knowledge of, 8, 10.
   Written deposit, 10.
Pharisee and Publican, 23, 125.
Pharisees :
   Admit women, 20.
   Affiliation with Scribes, 19.
   Aristocracy of learning, 19.
   Attitude toward Hellenism, 17.

Pharisees—*continued*—
Attribute work of Holy Spirit to the Devil, 150.
Belief in angels, 40.
Belief in future life, 39.
Brotherhood, 19, 20.
Cause of hostility to Christians, 58.
Champion Jesus, 64.
Children of the Devil, 153.
Collision with Jesus, 50.
Complacency, 125.
Conception of the Messiah, 40.
—— of Oral Law, 30.
—— of Righteousness, 122.
Demand signs, 86, 91, 119.
Disciples of Jesus, 63.
Division among, 63.
Doctrines, 3, 31.
Exponents of official Judaism, 23.
Fail to understand the Scriptures, 79.
Fear multitude, 63.
Formalists, 123.
Hated John the Baptist, 70.
Heirs of the past, 117.
Hypocrites, 133.
Idea of God and Man, 37.
Interesting historical study, 2.
Interpretation of ceremonial law, 44.
—— of Judaism, 21.
Interpreters of religion and life, 119.
Leaders of the people, 14, 17.
Literary Scorn for Jesus, 99.
Make void the Word of God by Tradition, 117.
Meaning of *Halachah*, 32.
Messianic Expectations, 12, 40.
Mock Jesus, 76.
Moderates, 37.
Must suppress Jesus or perish, 70.
Must be understood, 1.
Name, 12.

Nation, 22.
New Testament writers assume a knowledge, 11.
No gospel to the lost, 80.
Number, 20.
Official Rabbis, 3.
Origin of attitude towards the 'Am-ha-'arets, 22.
Origin in principle, 18.
Place of ecclesiastical eminence, 1.
Preservers of Traditional Judaism, 50.
Pride, 22, 47.
Problem, 8.
Properly seize the issue, 70.
Psalms, 77.
Rejected Jesus as the Messiah, 41, 43.
Religious leaders, 15.
—— party, 13.
—— teachers, 147.
Representatives of the Jewish Nation, 69.
Seclusive, 23.
Sect, 13.
Severe indictment, 116.
Share blame for death of Jesus, 102.
Some believe on Jesus, 64.
Source of knowledge of, 10.
Spiritually blind, 117, 118.
Spiritual pride, 22.
Stone Stephen, 147.
Theology, 3, 36.
Thieves and Robbers, 136.
Varieties:
The Shoulder Pharisee, 24.
The Wait-a-little Pharisee, 24.
The Bruised Pharisee, 24.
The Pestle Pharisee, 25.
The Ever-reckoning Pharisee, 25.
The Timid Pharisee, 26.
The God-loving Pharisee, 26.
Zeal to make proselytes, 142.

Philo, 42.
Philip, 150.
Phinehas, 25.
Phylacteries, 25, 26, 128.
Pick, 52, 53, 54, 56, 58, 99, 103, 105, 106, 107, 108, 119, 120, 128.
Piety, 47.
Pilate, 56, 62, 75, 99, 101, 146, 156, 157.
Plucking and eating wheat, 88.
Plummer, 9, 65, 74, 75, 79, 83, 89, 92, 96, 114, 127, 128, 132, 135.
Political Messiah, 41, 60, 99, 107, 112.
Polybius, 133.
Polytheism, 36.
Pompey, 15.
Pool of Bethesda, 86.
Power of life and death, 104.
Prejudice, 126.
Private fasts, 81.
Problem of divorce, 92.
Prophets, 28.
Psalms of Solomon, 9, 23, 39, 40, 42, 48, 76, 117.
Publican, 23.
Publicans and Sinners, 76 ff.
Public fasts, 81.
Purification, 44.
Pythagoreans, 5.

RABBAH, 34.
Rabban Jochanan ben Zakit, 37.
Rabbinical literature, 11, 59.
—— schools, 10, 93.
Rabbinic Judaism, 5, 6, 9, 59, 112.
Rabbinism, 77, 104.
Rabbis:
 Catalogue of rules, 87.
 Comments, 10.
 Conception of oral law, 30.
 Differ in views of the Messiah, 68.
 Emphasise outward form, 121.
 Interpret *Halachah*, 31.
 Later theology, 35.
 Masters of law, 30.

Never free from rules, 71.
Not content with Law of Moses, 46.
Puzzled, 87.
Rule of, 3.
Traditionalists, 130.
Rabbi Abahu, 55.
—— Aqiba, 41, 55, 95, 99.
—— ben Tema, 47.
—— Chasda, 118.
—— Dosithai, 36.
—— Drucker, 55, 56, 103.
—— Eleazer, 30.
—— Eliezer, 54, 143.
—— Jacob, 36.
—— Jechiel, 53.
—— Li'eser, 36.
—— Meir, 36.
—— Tarphon, 53, 136.
Real conflict, 72.
Rejection of God in rejecting Jesus, 72.
Religious Purification, 95.
Renan, 51.
Resurrection, 40.
Risen and Triumphant Christ, 157.
Robertson, J. M., 3.
Roman Catholicism, 25, 26.
—— Centurion, 63.
—— Emperor, 73.
Romanes, 113.
Romans, 11, 17, 40, 104, 107.
Roman wars, 15.
—— yoke, 15.
Ruler of the Synagogue, 138.
Rules for the Sabbath, 11, 85.

SABBATH, 48, 85.
Sabbatic Laws, 87.
—— River, 87.
Sadducees:
 Accused of hypocrisy, 134.
 Affiliation with priests, 19.
 Aristocracy of blood, 19.
 Chief priests, 68.
 Control High Priest, 17.

Sadducees—*continued*—
  Deny existence of angels, **40.**
  Deny a future life, 39.
  Expected no Messiah, 40.
  Hospitable to foreign influences, 17.
  Jesus warns disciples against, 137.
  Modern Calvinists, 37.
  Not mentioned in John's Gospel, 68.
  Possess great power, 19.
  Political party, 13.
  Question the resurrection, **94.**
Salome Alexandra, **14.**
Samaritans, 47.
Sanday, 49, 118.
Sanhedrin, 21, 56, 59, 62, 64, 67, 68, 70, 75, 76, 92, 94, 98, 99, 102, 104, 105, 106, 107, 108, 152, 157.
Sanscrit, 51.
Satan, 84, 149.
Schaefer, 85.
Schechter, 32, 33.
School of Hillel, 27, 28, 63, 93, 96.
—— of Shammai, 27, 28, 63, 93, 96.
Schuerer, 3, 19, 43, 46, 77, 87, 95, 142.
Schweitzer, **4, 49.**
Scotland, 20.
Scott, 2, 129.
Scribes, 18, 19, 30, 31, 44, 68, 71, 81, 95, 120, 130, 137.
Second Esdras, 10, 36, **48.**
Sects, 91 f.
Seitz, 41.
Septuagint, 133.
Sermon on the Mount, 120, **123,** 136, 141.
Seven woes, 140-146.
Shammai, 35-95.
Signs of the Times, 119.
Simeon, 50.
Simeon the Pharisee, **79.**
Simon Zelotes, 21.

Sinner, 77.
Sirach, 47.
Six illustrations, **122.**
Smith, 3, 87.
Son of God, 42, 87.
—— of Man, 42, 88, 102, **149.**
Sons of Gehinnom, 142.
Sparrow-Simpson, 102.
Spiritual blindness, 60, **99.**
Stanton, 42.
Stapfer, 52.
Stephen, 58, 59, 65, 103, 147.
Stoics, 4, 37.
Swete, 78, 92, 93, 95, 115, 130, **131.**
Sybilline Oracles, 41, 48.
Synagogue, 18, 43, 67, 90.
Synoptics, 11, 61, 66, 72, 87, 106, 131.

Taylor, 29.
Tertullian, 57.
Testaments of the Twelve Patriarchs, 9, 36, 43, 49, **122.**
Test. Levi, 43.
Thackeray, 124, 126.
Theological Schools, 100.
Theudas, 98.
Thomson, 12, 20, 21, 23, 40, 48, 49, 85.
Thorburn, 3.
Three woes for lawyers, **130.**
Tiberius, 108.
Tigranes, 15.
Timothy, 143, **144.**
Titus, 33, 55.
Tolstoi, 122.
Toy, **49.**
Tradition, 96, 144.
—— of the Elders, 10, 95, **104.**
—— supreme, 96.
Transmigration of souls, 39.
Trench, 78.
Trial before the Sanhedrin, **103.**
Tribute to Cæsar, 94.
Triumphal entry, **74.**
Trumpet, **134.**

Two kinds of labour on the Sabbath, 88.
Two ideas of righteousness, 120 f.
Tyndale, 144.

UNCLEAN CUP, 26, 123, 144.
Unitarians, 153.
Utica, 87.

VESPASIAN, 41.
Volz, 99.
Votaw, 151.
Vote of condemnation, 75.

WARFIELD, 159.
Washing of hands, 27, 93.
Weber, 32 f.
Weiss, 116.

Wellhausen, 51.
Wernle, 3, 5, 6.
Wesner, 85.
Westcott, 68, 70, 87, 95, 98, 100, 104, 107, 108, 118, 150, 153.
Wetstein, 114.
Whitewashing the sepulchre, 146.
Wilcken, 135.
William of Orange, 20.
Wilson, 103.
Winstanley, 49.
Worsley, 49.

ZACHARIAS, 50.
Zadokites, 13.
Zealots, 21, 98, 99, 122.
Zechariah, 48.
Zeus, 17.
Zimri, 25.

II.—INDEX OF SCRIPTURE PASSAGES AND OTHER QUOTATIONS

(1) New Testament

	PAGE
Matthew,	77
iii. 7,	62
iii. 7,	127
iii. 7,	133
iv. 6,	91
v.,	141
v. 15, 23,	133
v. 17 ff.,	120
v. 20,	121
v. 21-48,	122
v. 28,	25
vi.,	141
vi. 1-18,	120
vi. 1, 2,	134
vi. 2-7,	133
vi. 16,	81
vi. 16,	135
vi. 19-23,	26
vi. 25,	135
vi. 33,	121
vii.,	141
vii. 1 f.,	110
vii. 3,	136
vii. 3-5,	136
vii. 15,	26
vii. 15,	136
vii. 29,	3
viii. 19,	63
ix. 3,	71
ix. 6,	72, 73
ix. 10 ff.,	76, 80
ix. 13,	111, 114
ix. 14-17,	81
ix. 34,	83
xi. 16-19,	126, 128, 152
xi. 18,	128
xi. 19,	128

Matthew—	PAGE
xi. 21-24,	140
xi. 27,	154
xii. 1-14,	85
xii. 10,	89, 93
xii. 22-37,	83
xii. 31-33,	148
xii. 34,	66, 133
xii. 38,	91
xii. 38-45,	90
xiii. 13-17,	111, 116
xiii. 14,	116
xiii. 15,	116
xiii. 17,	116
xv. 1-20,	129
xv 1-30,	93
xv. 6,	130
xv. 7,	137
xv. 7-9,	133
xv. 10,	132
xv. 12,	94, 117, 132
xv. 12-20,	111
xv. 14,	117, 142
xv. 16-19,	132
xvi. 1,	90, 91, 119
xvi. 1-4,	111
xvi. 3,	119
xvi. 5-12,	133
xvi. 6,	137
xvi. 12,	137
xvi. 21,	152
xvii. 12,	151, 152
xvii. 42,	86
xviii. 7,	140
xix. 3,	69, 93
xix. 4,	144
xxi. 15 f.,	74
xxi. 26,	70

INDEX

Matthew—	PAGE
xxi. 40 f.,	155
xxi. 43,	104, 156
xxi. 44,	156
xxii. 29-33,	39
xxii. 41 f.,	155
xxiii.,	61, 138, 140
xxiii. 2,	1
xxiii. 3,	2, 25
xxiii. 3-6,	25
xxiii. 4,	2, 38
xxiii. 5,	126
xxiii. 13-39,	133
xxiii. 13-32,	140
xxiii. 14-22,	140
xxiii. 15,	20
xxiii. 16-22,	142
xxiii. 13,	126
xxiii. 23 f.,	143
xxiii. 25, 26,	144
xxiii. 27, 28,	146
xxiii. 29-33,	141, 146
xxiii. 33,	66
xxiii. 37,	159
xxiv. 5, 23 f.,	98
xxiv. 30,	92
xxv. 46,	39
xxvi. 59,	102
xxvi. 60,	102
xxvi. 61,	102
xxvi. 63 f.,	75
xxvi. 64,	75, 92
xxvi. 65,	71
xxvi. 67 f.,	105
xxvii. 11,	106
xxvii. 13,	105
xxvii. 17-25,	104
xxvii. 18,	107
xxvii. 25,	156
xxvii. 37 f.,	102
xxvii. 43,	76
xxvii. 62-66,	101
xxvii. 63 f.,	97
xxvii. 64,	101
Mark—	95
i. 21-28,	63, 86

Mark—	PAGE
i. 27,	71
ii. 7,	148
ii. 10,	72
ii. 12,	72
ii. 15 ff.,	76
ii. 16,	78
ii. 18,	82, 93, 128
ii. 18-22,	81
ii. 23,	85
ii. 24,	93
iii. 5,	89, 111, 115
iii. 6,	85
iii. 19-30,	83
iii. 22,	93
iii. 28-30,	148
iv. 11,	116
iv. 12,	111, 116
vi. 43,	93
vi. 45-56,	93
vii.,	28
vii. 1-23,	93, 129
vii. 3,	94
vii. 5,	130
vii. 6,	137
vii. 6-7,	133
vii. 8,	130
vii. 9,	30, 131
vii. 13,	132
vii. 14,	132
vii. 17,	117, 132
vii. 19,	132
viii. 11,	90, 91, 119
viii. 11-13,	111
viii. 12,	92, 119
viii. 14-21,	133
viii. 15,	137
viii. 18,	70
x. 2,	69, 93
xii. 13,	94
xii. 24-27,	39
xiii. 10,	116
xiii. 21 f.,	98
xiv. 55,	102
xiv. 58,	102
xiv. 61 f.,	75

THE PHARISEES AND JESUS

Mark—	PAGE
xiv. 62,	92
xiv. 64,	71
xiv. 65,	105
xv. 2,	105
xv. 3,	105
xv. 9-14,	104
xv. 10,	156
xv. 13,	147
xv. 29,	102
xv. 30,	103
Luke i. 1-4,	62
ii. 11,	42
ii. 37-54,	120
ii. 46,	120
iii. 7,	62, 65, 133
iv. 9 f.,	91
iv. 31-7,	86
iv. 17-26,	28, 71
v. 24,	72
v. 29 ff.,	76
v. 33-39,	81
v. 39,	111, 114
vi. 1-11,	85
vi. 7,	89, 115
vi. 11,	89
vi. 20-26,	140
vi. 24-26,	121
vi. 37 f.,	110
vi. 37-42,	133
vi. 41 f.,	136
vii. 3,	63
vii. 29,	76
vii. 29-30,	127
vii. 29-35,	126
vii. 30,	70
vii. 30-33,	82
vii. 34,	79, 82, 128
vii. 36,	79
vii. 36-50,	63
vii. 37,	77
viii. 10,	111, 116
ix. 57-60,	24
ix. 61 f.,	24
x. 22,	154
xi.,	140

Luke—	PAGE
xi. 14-36,	83
xi. 14-38,	85
xi. 15,	83
xi. 16-32,	90, 92
xi. 37-54,	63, 93, 96, 111
xi. 39 f.,	26, 123, 145
xi. 39-44,	143
xi. 42,	143
xi. 42-44,	140
xi. 43,	124
xi. 44,	146
xi. 46-52,	140
xi. 47,	146
xi. 52,	141
xi. 52-54,	119
xii.,	138
xii. 1,	138
xii. 1, 2,	133
xii. 3,	138
xii. 10,	148
xiii. 1,	99
xiii. 10-17,	138
xiii. 10-21,	85, 90
xiii. 15-17,	133
xiii. 31 ff.,	64
xiv. 1,	90
xiv. 1-24,	63, 85
xiv. 7,	124
xv. 1,	80
xv. 1-32,	76
xv. 25-32,	129
xvi. 14,	124
xvi. 15,	124
xvi. 31,	91
xvi. 54,	120
xvii. 20 f.,	64
xviii.,	23
xviii. 1-14,	120
xviii. 9,	125
xviii. 12,	81
xviii. 13,	23
xix. 7,	77
xix. 39,	74
xx. 34-40,	39
xx. 35,	105

INDEX

Luke—	PAGE	Luke—	PAGE
xxii. 63-65,	105	xxiii. 2,	104, 105
xxii. 71,	75	xxiii. 3,	106
xxiii.,	104	xxiii. 34,	109

The Logia or Q

Matthew—	PAGE	John—	PAGE
xi. 16-19	62	vi. 44, 64 f.,	111
xi. 21-23,	62	vi. 52,	151, 152
xii.,	62	vii.,	61
Luke—		vii. 12,	98
vii. 29-35,	62	vii. 14-30,	97
x. 13-15,	62	vii. 15,	98, 99
xi.,	62	vii. 17,	100, 127
John—		vii. 19,	152
i. 19-24,	63	vii. 20,	128
i. 19-26,	70	vii. 27,	42
i. 26, 29-37,	66	vii. 31,	91
ii. 6,	95	vii. 34,	152
ii. 18-22,	66	vii. 35 f.,	152
ii. 18, 20,	67	vii. 47,	100
ii. 19,	69, 102, 152	vii. 48,	151
ii. 19-22,	102	vii. 49,	22, 77
iii.,	68	vii. 50-53,	64
iii. 1-14,	111	viii. 9, 16,	28
iii. 2,	68, 112	viii. 13,	100
iii. 9,	112	viii. 14,	101
iii. 10,	113	viii. 19,	101
iii. 19,	111	viii. 20,	85
iv. 1-4,	66, 152	viii. 21,	153
iv. 27,	25	viii. 21-52,	151
v.,	85, 87, 88	viii. 25,	153
v. 16,	86	viii. 30 f.,	27
v. 17 f.,	87	viii. 31,	63
v. 18,	71	viii. 32,	123
v. 18,	73, 151	viii. 36,	123
v. 19-47,	73	viii. 40-44,	153
v. 31 ff.,	100	viii. 46 f.,	154
v. 35,	70	viii. 48,	84, 128
v. 39,	126	ix.,	85, 89
v. 40,	126	ix. 16,	64
v. 41-43,	152	ix. 16, 31,	77
v. 42 f.,	151	ix. 22, 34,	64
vi. 14 f.,	41, 106	ix. 24,	77
vi. 30,	91	ix. 29,	101

THE PHARISEES AND JESUS

John—	PAGE
ix. 39,	118
ix. 40 f.,	111, 118
x. 1-21,	186
x. 19-21,	28, 64
x. 20,	128
x. 21,	84
x. 22-42,	71
x. 25-38,	151
x. 26 f.,	154
x. 33,	73
x. 38,	154
xi. 45-53,	91
xi. 47 f.,	155
xi. 48,	104
xii. 9-11,	91
xii. 19,	64, 74
xii. 34,	42
xii. 42,	28, 64
xiii. 27,	147
xviii. 8-30,	104
xviii. 31,	104
xviii. 33,	106
xix. 1-15,	104
xix. 6,	75
xix. 6-12,	107
xix. 12,	108
xix. 15,	108
xix. 38-40,	64
Acts—	
iv. 1-3,	58
v. 28,	157
v. 33-42,	58, 98
v. 34,	19, 21
vi. 2,	103
vi. 9-14,	58
vi. 14,	104

Acts—	PAGE
vii. 52,	147
vii. 59,	147
x.,	132
x. 14,	95
x. 28,	47
xi. 3,	78
xviii. 12-16,	105
xxi. 38,	99
xxiii. 3,	146
xxiii. 6,	19
xxiii. 6-9,	21
xxiii. 8,	40
Romans—	
ii. 19,	117
ix. 1-3,	60
x.,	60
xi.,	60
xi. 22,	147
2 Corinthians—	
iii. 15,	159
xi. 13,	136
Galatians—	
ii. 15,	77
iii. 23,	18
Ephesians—	
ii. 14-17,	19
iv. 18,	115
1 Timothy—	
i. 4,	33
iv. 7,	33
Titus—	
i. 14,	33
Hebrews—	
xii. 29,	147
James,	123
2 Peter,	136

(2) OLD TESTAMENT

Exodus—	PAGE
xxi.,	34
xxi. 17,	150
xxxi.,	34
Leviticus—	
xi. 4, 42 f.,	144
xix. 18,	20

Leviticus—	PAGE
xxi. 10,	75
xxiv. 16,	75
xxvii. 30,	143
Numbers—	
xv. 30 f.,	149
xv. 38,	31

INDEX

Deuteronomy—	PAGE
xiv. 22 f.,	143
xxi. 6,	156
1 Samuel—	
iii. 14,	149
1 Kings—	
xviii. 38,	92
xxi. 10, 13,	75
2 Kings—	
i. 10 ff.,	92
Ezra—	
ix. 1 f.,	22
x. 2, 11,	22
Nehemiah—	
x.,	28
x. 28-31,	22
Job—	
xxxiv. 30,	134
xxxvi. 13,	134
Psalms—	
i.,	78, 155
xxvi. 6,	156
liv.,	155
lxxiii. 13,	156
lxxii., 6,	74
cvi. 3,	123

Psalms—	PAGE
cx.,	155
cxviii.,	130
cxix. 126,	130
Isaiah—	
v.,	140
vi. 9-10,	116
ix. 6,	42
xxix. 13,	131, 137
lviii. 2,	123
Lamentations—	
iv. 20,	42
Ezekiel—	
xxii. 27,	136
Daniel—	
xii. 2,	40
Hosea—	
vi. 6,	79, 114
Amos—	
vi. 6,	144
Micah—	
v. 2,	42
Zephaniah—	
iii. 3,	136
Zechariah—	
xiii. 2,	98, 136

APOCRYPHA

2 Ezra—	
vii. 50,	150
Tobit—	
vi. 14,	24
xii. 8,	123
Sirach—	
xxxviii. 24-26,	47

1 Maccabees—	
i.,	17
ii.,	17
ii. 27,	21
ii, 44, 48,	78
vii. 9,	13

APOCALYPSES

Enoch—	
xlvii. 3,	41
xlviii. 2,	42
cv. 2,	42
Baruch—	
xv. 7, 8,	150
Assumption of Moses,	99

Book of Jubilees, 50,	45
Psalms of Solomon—	
ii. 38-41,	23
iii. 16,	40
iv. 7,	134
xiii. 5-11,	23
xiii. 9 f.,	40

Psalms of Solomon—	PAGE		PAGE
xiv. 1, . . .	23	Testament of the Twelve	
xvii. 16, 26, . .	23	Patriarchs, . . .	122
xvii. 23-30, . .	42	Testament of Levi—	
xvii. 35 f., . .	42	viii. 14, . . .	43
xvii. 41, . . .	42	Sybilline Oracles—	
xvii. 50, . . .	117	vv. 285 f., . .	41

TALMUD

1. Zera'im—
    Berachoth, fol. iv. col. 2, 130
        ,,   ,, vi. ,, 1, 34
    Jer. ,,   ,, ix. ,, 7, 25
        ,,   ,, xiii. 25
        ,,   ,, xliii.a, 97
      ,, —R. ,, xliv. 150
    Tal. Maaser, ,, i. ,, 1, 143
        ,,   ,, iv. ,, 5, 143
2. Mo'edh—
    Tract. Shabbath in Mishna, 46
    Shabbath, fol. xxii. 6, . 45
        ,,   ,, xxix. 1, . 32
        ,,   ,, xxxi. 1, . 35
        ,,   ,, civ. b, . 54
    Jer. ,,   ,, cvii., . 144
        ,,   ,, cxvi. 1, . 53
    Erubin, ,, xxi. 2, 30, 130
    b. Jona, ,, lxvi. d, . 55
    b. Succ., ,, xx. a, . 18
    Ros. Hash., ,, xvii. b, . 142
    Taanith, ,, xxiv. a, . 143
    j. ,, ,, lxv. b, . 55
    B. Meg., ,, lxxxvi. d, 34
    B. Moed. qat., ,, i. a, . 146
3. Nashim—
    M. Jeb., ,, iv. 13, . 55
    b. Gitt., ,, lvi. b, . 55
        ,, ,, lvii. a, . 55
    Sotah, ,, iv., . 44
        ,, ,, ix., . 5
    Bab. ,, ,, xxi. 2, . 25
    ,, ,, ,, xxii. b, 24, 134
    ,, ,, ,, xxii. 1, . 25
    Tal. Kidd, ,, lxxi. a, . 143
4. Nezikin—
    Kama Baba, fol. iv., . 34
        ,,   ,, lii. a, . 118
    T. Sanh., ,, ix. 7, . 56
    M. ,, ,, x. 2, . 55
    T. ,, ,, x. 11, . 55
        ,, ,, xi. 3, 30, 44, 130
    b. ,, ,, xliii. a, . 56
    b. ,, ,, lxvii. a, . 55
        ,, ,, ciii. a, . 55
    b. ,, ,, cvi., . 55
        ,, ,, cvii. b, 5, 55
    Maccoth, ,, xxiii. 2, . 32
    Aboth, Mishna, . 28, 30
        ,, ,, i. 15, . 35
        ,, ,, i. 16, . 35
        ,, ,, ii. 2, . 37
        ,, ,, ii. 4, 20, 100
    ,, Tal., ,, ii. 8, . 150
        ,, ,, ii. 14, . 36
        ,, ,, iii. 10, . 36
        ,, ,, iii 12, . 36
        ,, ,, iii. 20, . 95
        ,, ,, v. 18, . 38
        ,, ,, v. 20, 39, 47
    ,, Nathan ,, xxxvii., . 25
5. Kodhashim—
    Erach, ,, xvi. b, . 136
6. Teharoth—
    Tract. Kelim., . . 46
    Mikwaoth, fol. iv. 1, 95
    Niddah, ,, iv. 2, 29

INDEX

LATE MIDRASH

	PAGE
Shem. R., fol. xxx.,	87

POST TALMUDIC TRACT

Sopherim, fol. xvi. 6,	44

TALMUDIC TRACT

b. Kallah, fol. li. a,.	55

BABYLONIAN TRACT

Ab. Zar., fol. xvii. a,	77
b. A. Zar., fol. iii. b,	29

PHILO

Alleg., chap. i. 46,	87

JOSEPHUS

	PAGE		PAGE
Antiq., book ii. chap. viii. 14,	20	Antiq., book xv. chap. x, 4,	5
,, ,, iv. ,, viii. 16,	156	,, ,, xvii. ,, ii. 4,	47
,, ,, xiii. ,, vii. 9,	12	,, ,, xvii. ,, x. 7,	98
,, ,, xiii. ,, x. 5-6,	12	,, ,, xviii. ,, i. 1,	21
,, ,, xiii. ,, x. 6,	38	,, ,, xviii. ,, i. 3,	30
,, ,, xiii. ,, x. 6,	48	,, ,, xviii. ,, i. 3,	37
,, ,, xiii. ,, xi.,	18	,, ,, xviii. ,, i. 3,	39
,, ,, xiii. ,, xiii. 5,	14	,, ,, xviii. ,, i. 3,	44
,, ,, xiii. ,, xiv. 2,	13	,, ,, xviii. ,, i. 4,	19
,, ,, xiii. ,, xv. 5,	14	,, ,, xviii. ,, iii. 3,	40
,, ,, xiii. ,, xvi. 2,	14	,, ,, xx. ., viii. 6,	99
,, ,, xiv. ,, i. 1,	14	,, ,, xx. ,, ix. 1,	17
,, ,, xiv. ,, i. 2-4,	15	,, ,, xx. ,, ix. 1,	19
,, ,, xiv. ,, ii.-v.,	15	Wars, ,, v. ,, i.,	21
,, ,, xiv. ,, iv. 2,	46	,, ,, ii. ,, viii. 14,	5
,, ,, xiv. ,, vii. 4,	16	,, ,, ii. ,, viii. 14,	37
,, ,, xiv. ,, viii.,	16	,, ,, ii. ,, viii. 14,	38
,, ,, xiv. ,, xi.-xiii.,	16	,, ,, ii. ,, viii. 14,	39
,, ,, xiv. ,, xiii.,	16	,, ,, vi. ,, v. 4,	41
,, ,, xiv. ,, xiii. 10,	16	,, ,, vii. ,, v. 1,	87
,, ,, xiv. ,, xiv.-xv.,	16	Life,	2, 5
,, ,, xv. ,, i. 4,	16		

www.ingramcontent.com/pod-product-compliance
Lightning Source LLC
Chambersburg PA
CBHW051925160426
43198CB00012B/2042